Cryptocurrency Mastery: 5 Expert Secrets, Mastering Bitcoin, Mastering Ethereum, Blockchain Technology

Anthony Tu

information contained within this document, including, but not limited to, —errors, omissions, or inaccuracies

For more information, go to

www.wonpublications.com

About the Author

Anthony Tu (also known as Anthony Tuanga) is a computer scientist, author and a cryptocurrency investor. He has been working in the field of computer science for the last 10 years and completed his degree at Harvard University. He came across cryptocurrencies early in 2011 and fell in love with the technology.

He is a large investor in cryptocurrencies such as Bitcoin, Ethereum and continues to share his vast knowledge in the space.

Outside of work, he is a family man. He loves to spend time with his beautiful wife and son.

Table of Contents

11

Cryptocurrency: 5 Expert Secrets for Beginners: Investing into Bitcoin, Ethereum and Litecoin.

Introduction

I want to thank you for choosing this book, *'Cryptocurrency: 5 Expert Secrets for Beginners: Investing into Bitcoin, Ethereum and Litecoin - Bitcoin, Blockchain, Ethereum, Cryptocurrency, and Litecoin.'* I know you'll find this book valuable on your journey to learning about cryptocurrencies. If you really find this book helpful, please leave an honest review on Amazon.

Cryptocurrencies are a craze right now, and they present an attractive investment opportunity for anyone with some extra cash. Cryptocurrencies are gaining more and more legitimacy as they are legalized, and regulatory authorities are stepping in to maintain order.

Cryptocurrencies are the new means of exchange that only function in the digital world. It's a whole new monetary system that is entirely different from the one we are used it. It is based on cryptography, digital signatures and addresses to conduct transactions. These transactions help keep the users anonymous, which protects their privacy from the eyes of the state. That doesn't mean these cryptocurrencies are always used for illegal dealings – there is a central ledger to most of these currencies, which helps make transactions traceable without giving information on the users.

2009 was the year when cryptocurrencies truly took off. It was all because of Satoshi Nakamoto – the founder of the famous cryptocurrency known as Bitcoin. He came up with a decentralized system where peer-to-peer networking was used to conduct transactions instead of a central figure directing everything.

Bitcoin is the most famous cryptocurrency right now, but thanks to its technology, thousands of other similar currencies have also cropped up. These cryptocurrencies are known as altcoins. A lot of them are just poor copies of Bitcoin, but some have made modifications and updates to make the technology even better. This includes Litecoin, Ethereum, Ripple and Dogecoin.

When it comes to investing in these cryptocurrencies, many people have a lot of doubts and questions. They aren't sure about the risks involved, and are confused by the rumors they have heard. The aim of this book is to solve this problem.

In this book, we will first familiarize you with the concepts of cryptocurrency, explain the various benefits and risks that come with it, and tell you five secrets you need to follow while investing.

Let's get started!

Chapter One: Basics of Cryptocurrency

Cryptocurrency is the name given to any digital currency that is deemed secure because of cryptography — or a particular kind of encryption method that's perfect for the whole blockchain process. What's amazing about cryptocurrencies is that no central authorities govern them. They are organic and are a perfect system on their own. The government or anyone not involved in Blockchain cannot manipulate them in any way— keeping your funds always in check. In fact, it is virtually impossible for any governing body to track down any transactions and associate it to an individual. This is what makes cryptocurrencies so fascinating and why some governments are highly against cryptocurrencies.

One thing about cryptocurrency transactions is that they might be used for illicit activities — such as tax evasion or even money laundering. Prior to larger adoption in 2017, particularly the early years, there has been a lot of controversy about the uses of cryptocurrencies, that it is only used for activity done on dark web, including drug dealings.

This is different in 2017 where there has been a larger acceptance of cryptocurrencies, with some banks incorporating the Blockchain technology and various companies accepting cryptocurrencies as a form of payment. The main argument towards cryptocurrencies is the ability for parties to easily send and accept funds from each other, even in cryptocurrency form, and only with minimal transaction fees. There are also many other uses for cryptocurrency, including crowdfunding and online voting. After all, people find it easier to spend online currencies instead of real ones— they don't cause too much hassle either.

Cryptocurrency is money created by the use of encryption techniques of advanced computer programming. These same techniques are used to carry out and verify the transfer of funds. Cryptocurrencies are independent of central banks and are decentralized. This means that parties can send and receive funds directly towards each other without a middleman. For most people, sending money is a hassle, particularly when you want to send money abroad. If you're transferring money between local banks, it could potentially take days for the banks to clear and verify the transactions to be made. When sending abroad, this is a different case; in certain situations this could take more than a week, let alone the fees of processing the transactions. Some major companies like Western Union allow faster transactions, but it comes at a cost, the fees. Welcome Bitcoin.

In 2009, Bitcoin became the first practicable cryptocurrency, proving that a decentralized currency could exist. This is ironic; given that Bitcoin inventor Satoshi Nakamoto never set out to create a new form of money. He wanted to solve the problem of centralized digital cash and created a peer-to-peer digital cash system. He ended up developing Bitcoin, an entirely unregulated form of currency, which relied upon extensive mathematical computations to validate authenticity. It was with the birth of

Bitcoin that cryptocurrency became a reality, forever changing how we do transactions.

The implications of cryptocurrency are so great that some central banks have attempted to involve themselves in the technology, with some attempting to issue their own cryptocurrencies. However, the currency they produce is not officially considered cryptocurrency as they can only develop centralized money. The idea behind decentralization is to allow the open market to influence the power. With centralization, all the power and control is with the centralized body, the central banks, meaning that you and I have no say in how much money is created or what it's worth. In this sense, the Federal Reserve can manipulate the value of traditional currencies (i.e US Dollar) via printing more money and there's nothing we can do. The proponents of cryptocurrency are very keen on keeping the "true" digital currency decentralized and because of this, cryptocurrencies have seen to be very favorable. Because of the unique nature of cryptocurrencies, is it actually deflationary, as time goes on, the value of most cryptocurrencies will go higher.

Rise of Cryptocurrency

Cryptocurrencies, such as Bitcoin, Ethereum, Litecoin and others, have had a lot of publicity, particularly in 2017. This is primarily due to the large exposure given by the news, social media and financial institutions. As the levels of financial/digital literacy of the general population have increased, cryptocurrency acceptance has also made leaps in purchasing power. In 2010, a Bitcoin investor, known as Laslo, claimed to have purchased two pizzas for roughly 10,000 Bitcoins. It was considered the first instance where a cryptocurrency was used to make a purchase. At the time, Bitcoins were virtually worthless. As of November 2017, Bitcoin is valued higher than gold, with one-coin worth nearly $10,000!

At first, most were very skeptical of Bitcoin and its technology, seeing it as a form of counterfeit or a device of criminals. This was particularly so when it was publicized as the means of trade on the 'Silk Road,' a part of the dark Internet where all sorts of unsavory behavior were rampant.

However, there is now an increasing involvement of legitimate business and government with cryptocurrency. New applications and even ATM's are incorporated to allow cryptocurrency transactions to occur. As a consequence, the market capitalization of all cryptocurrencies is more than $250,000,000,000!

By Mid 2017, we have seen a rise in cryptocurrencies, revealing more than 1000 cryptocurrencies. Most people have heard of Bitcoin, especially since recent ransomware attacks have demanded payment in Bitcoins. The benefit to criminals of this is that any such payment by a victim would be untraceable.

If the website for coinmarketcap is checked, it will be seen that there is a small graph beside the type of cryptocurrency, each showing the movement of the currency in the last week, as well as the percentage change in the last 24 hours. It will be seen that there is a significant disparity in the values of the various cryptocurrencies with one Bitcoin being worth nearly $10,000 and a total market capitalization of more than $150,000,000,000. Another cryptocurrency called Bytecoin was worth less than one cent although the total capitalization of Bytecoins was more than $200,000,000. Some cryptocurrencies have small capitalizations. An example is MikeTheMug cryptocurrency with a capitalization of approximately $1000! Just reading this, you may be wondering how a coin like 'MikeTheMug' can be taken seriously, and with all due respect for MikeTheMug, it is actually easier than most people think to create and issue a coin, which makes some individuals quite skeptical about cryptocurrencies.

Though there are a lot of valid and exciting potential projects within cryptocurrencies, it should be noted there are also a lot of 'joke' coins with no actual fundamental value. A good example is Dogecoin that I myself do find quite hysterical, however, the coin itself serves no real purpose aside from representing the patriotism that society has created through hysterical memes and the Internet. To put that in perspective, Dogecoin has a market cap of more than $200,000,000, based on a meme of a dog.

We will have more to say about the quality and worth of cryptocurrencies later.

Cryptocurrency as Money

The people involved in cryptocurrency call the currencies we use, in everyday life, 'fiat', or 'fiat currency' Despite the word 'currency' in the word cryptocurrency, there are greater similarities between cryptocurrencies and stocks than cryptocurrencies and fiat currencies. A purchase of some cryptocurrency is similarly a purchase of a technology stock, an entry in a digital ledger called a blockchain, and a part of the digital network for that cryptocurrency. Buying cryptocurrencies is similarly to stock purchasing because each 'cryptocurrency' represents a different project. When you purchase these cryptocurrencies, you're buying a share within the project. An example of which is Ethereum or Ether. Having Ether allows the investor to participate in voting within the Ethereum network.

Cryptocurrency is a means of exchange that uses cryptography so that transactions are secure. They are used to exercise control over the manufacture of further units of the currency. Cryptocurrencies are a type of what is called alternative currencies; different from traditional currencies such as everyone is familiar with, the US Dollar, the Euro, the British Pound, etc.

Due to their frequent and great fluctuations in value, one of the two fundamentals of money, namely "a store of value" is lacking. Within any new markets, there are large fluctuations in the prices of the assets. But as the market begins to grow over time, you will see price stability as well as more institutional and commercial uses. A good example is the stock market within periods of recessions, where uncertainty generally leads to large fluctuations in prices. However, most of the time, the prices of the large capitalization companies in the stock market are fairly stable. Within the cryptocurrency market, Bitcoin is starting to unfold as the most stable cryptocurrency.

Quite ironically, Bitcoin was initially released to allow decentralized peer-to-peer transactions to take place, but because of the explosive popularity of Bitcoin in recent years, Bitcoin has seen to become more of a store value due to ridiculous costs to transfer Bitcoin in between wallets. A lot of individuals see Bitcoin as the gold standard within the cryptocurrency world, and much like gold is to be held, a lot of investors choose to hold Bitcoin within the cryptocurrency market. Some digital currencies exhibit the behavior of countries having significant inflation in that value is not retained.

Chapter Two: Important Terminology

Blockchain

Blockchain is what encompasses all transactions of cryptocurrencies, most prominently Bitcoin. The blockchain is a public record that solely exists in the digital world— which means you wouldn't get any physical coins of any sort. If you need to buy something online, and you're allowed to pay cryptocurrencies for it, then you will be able to get that item even without real cash— as long as you have enough cryptocurrency.

One of the main things about Blockchain is that it allows you to have this sense of ownership over something, even if you do not have it in your hands, and you also have the capacity to transfer ownership to someone else when you get the proper Blockchain record done. You can think of it like an online storage, where information is stored on a network and that network tracks all information. You also have to realize that once a transaction is done, then it is there forever. What happens in the Blockchain stays in the Blockchain— and that's how it will always be.

You can get cryptocurrencies either by accepting, trading or mining for them. When it comes to mining, you can think of it as how mining is done in real life— or the way of looking for what it is you need. In this case, the computer will be the one doing the mining and will be working through complex situations to help you find what you are looking for.

Miners will then make use of a collection of transactions by organizing them in one block alone. Now, with the help of these blocks— and information— the chain (Blockchain) gets to be created, which means that there will no longer be any kind of inconsistencies. There won't be any bad or bouncing checks or anything that would make transactions full of hassle. Self-Regulation is also easily done, as blockchain systems make regular inspections to make way for secure transactions because several confirmations are done before a transaction is made— safer than your usual bank or remittance transactions.

What you have to understand about Blockchain is that one computer alone does not just handle transactions— there is no "central" or "main" bank here. They are managed by distributed nodes or pathways that are then in charge of having copies of everything that happens in the blockchain, together with the users who have created those records, so that copies will be synchronized and will easily be understood by the system— making transactions seamless and easy.

So, for example, your Bitcoins are all lined up in one row, so even if they are not currently in use, the Blockchain can make something out of them, always keeping them in check, and always keeping you and other users as top priority. Transactions are also not done on standard systems— specialized hardware is used for them.

Many people believe that in the future, more people would be making use of the Blockchain system, in particular with the emergence of many companies online, mostly those that employ amazing technology. With the help of a great transaction ledger, such as blockchain, it might be used by international communications systems— to make sure that transactions become safer and easier to do.

If you like to know more about Blockchain Technology,

Visit Amazon.com, and search the following book code,

B077C5CX9J

Bitcoin

One of the first digital currencies around was created back in 2009. The infamous Satoshi Nakamoto, who, even today is suspected of being perhaps more than one person, created Bitcoin. It was created as a means to provide a new way of making online payments and transactions, which is not operated by the government and is decentralized— you will learn more about it in the succeeding chapter of this book! As of November 2017, the total of Bitcoins has amounted to over 16.6 million, which means that it would be a whopping $150 billion in market value.

What you can keep in mind now is that you will never be able to hold Bitcoins physically and that they are operated by private keys— or strings of letters and numbers that are linked by an encrypted algorithm. For this, you would be using a public key— like one of those bank account numbers, which would then act as the address of your transaction. As we mentioned earlier, all transactions involving Bitcoin and other cryptocurrencies are based on the Blockchain. A simpler way of putting it is if you imagine the blockchain as a storage for all your Bitcoin. These private keys are given to you and act as a password for your Bitcoin information on the Blockchain. It's much like a key to a vault, however it is online; meaning nothing can be physically touched.

There are advantages and disadvantages to this. The biggest advantage is the level of liquidity and the layer of protection. It allows you to move around funds almost instantaneously. The peer-to-peer transaction on the blockchain allows individuals to send Bitcoin (and other cryptocurrencies) to each other in the matter of minutes, anywhere in the world. Additionally, having everything stored online allows protection in case something happens to you physically, if your house gets burnt down, robbery, etc. That being said, it leaves you vulnerable to cyber-attacks.

There are also two ways of writing Bitcoin. Bitcoin, with a capitalized B, talks about the concept or identity of cryptocurrencies, while Bitcoin, with a small letter b, is about the amount of currency being used. It could also be abbreviated to BTC (Bitcoin Transaction). Sometimes, the letters XBT are also used.

A lot of people say that Bitcoin stands out from the rest because of its extremely safe online ledger that cannot be accessed by hackers, making you confident that no one will be able to copy your data because only private keys are used for this. This being said, the protection of your Bitcoin is solely based on your ability to keep your private keys safe. If you lose the private keys, you hypothetically lose the key to your house, and given that nature of the online world, be cautious where you store your private keys.

TIP:

Write down your private key somewhere offline and hide it somewhere you can find. This will protect you in case something happens, such as a computer virus.

If you like to know more about Bitcoin

Visit Amazon.com, and search the following book code,

B076DF24SD

Mining

Contrary to the given name, Bitcoin Mining is not like traditional mining; Bitcoin Mining is the primary process of adding and verifying transactions so they can be placed in the blockchain. The sole purpose of this is so that new Bitcoin can also be released. Anyone, as long as the person has reliable Internet access, could try mining for Bitcoins or any other cryptocurrencies.

Back in the day, regular desktop CPUs were used for mining, but these days, due to large demand, Graphic Processing Units (GPUs) are mostly used, together with Application Specific Integrated Circuit (ASIC), hardware that's designed specifically for the process of mining Bitcoins. The dramatic increase in the price of Bitcoin lead to the increase in the demand for stronger computers. This has caused a problem in the computer industry, raising the value of GPUs. As Bitcoin was increasing up to $10,000 per coin, people tried to get into mining in order to capture 'free' Bitcoins, however, this was seen to be counterproductive as the price of electricity to mine for the Bitcoin outweighed the price of obtaining Bitcoin.

What happens during a mining session is that recent transactions are compiled so that a puzzle can potentially be solved in the right manner, and once that puzzle is solved, then Bitcoins can be released. It's like a contest where the first person that guesses right will then win Bitcoins, as a prize, also known as block rewards. The difficulty of puzzles depends on the kind of effort that's introduced in the network and is adjusted per week— to make sure that no one will cheat, and block rewards will be given only to those who deserve them. Block Rewards also stand for each block that has been mined, which could then be halved every four years— or for every 210,000 blocks. These will then be used for transaction fees, so you will not have to pay extra.

Ethereum

One of the newest parts of the blockchain is Ethereum, which has gained large popularity in 2017, becoming the second most traded cryptocurrency. Ethereum is a software platform that's decentralized which was released in 2015. It is something that enables distributed applications and smart contacts to be built without control, downtime, or any form of fraud. So more than just being a part of blockchain, Ethereum also acts as a programming language that completely runs on the blockchain, and is responsible for helping developers improve and publish more blockchain mechanisms— so that the future of blockchain will certainly be brighter.

In short, Ethereum acts the same as Bitcoin, with a decentralized system, faster transaction time and lower transaction costs, however, the major difference is that Ethereum is a project with an ambitious team which aims to change the way Blockchain technology is implemented in society. Ethereum focuses on projects that allow the use of blockchain technology within different industries, particularly industries that are based on peer-to-peer transactions. A good example is the secondhand car industry. Instead of the nitty-gritty government document/fees and waiting times, the application of blockchain technology would allow individuals to do direct peer-to-peer transactions, without the need for government intervention like check-ups, finances and other documents. This is because information would be stored on the blockchain so government approval wouldn't be needed to confirm transactions, thus lowering transaction times.

What you have to understand about applications that run on this platform is that they are mostly used by people who are trying to develop new apps. So, currencies can be exchanged, and work can easily be monetized, decentralized, and be secure so that trying to access the system won't be too hard for those who need and are allowed to access it.

If you like to know more about Bitcoin

Visit Amazon.com, and search the following book code,

B076W27PT6

Litecoin

With a market cap of over $ 5,000,000,000 as of November 2017, Litecoin deems itself to be the second best CryptoCurrency program out there - second to Bitcoin, much like the silver to gold. Litecoin transactions happen in a fast and secure manner, in fact, Litecoin is significantly faster and cheaper than its predecessor, Bitcoin — perfect for those who hate waiting a little too long just to send or receive money. Specialized and safe computer hardware is also used to make this happen.

A former Google employee by the name of Charlie Lee released Litecoin on Github in 2011. The main difference between Bitcoin and Litecoin is the time taken to process a block. Litecoin reduces the time taken to 2.5 minutes, while Bitcoin still takes 10 minutes. The Litecoin network has also been programmed to produce four times as many currency units as Bitcoin, making Litecoin four times faster.

Other Cryptocurrencies

There are more than 1000 different cryptocurrencies, so it seems like common sense that there are a large variety of cryptocurrencies out there. Given the increased popularity that took place in 2017, there has been a lot of new and vastly different cryptocurrencies issued, some which have no real practical purpose to society, and some that could potentially change the world. So when it comes to investing in cryptocurrencies, always do your research. There are many different types of cryptocurrencies out there, but the fascinating aspect of cryptocurrencies is not the fact that it's centralized but the innovative technology that is occurring since the introduction of Bitcoin.

A good example is Ripple. While Ripple is a unique example in the cryptocurrency world, its primary aims to increase the efficiency of large scale transactions. The primary users of the Ripple network are banks and financial institutions where companies such as Visa and MasterCard charge higher fees upon transactions. Ripple is much cheaper than its competitors with fees almost nonexistent and transactions almost instantaneous.

Another good example is OmiseGO. Based on the Ethereum network, OmiseGO aims to improve transactions between Asian countries. Their goal is to eliminate the troubling financial sector and problems associated with large-scale transactions between trades. Additionally, the company Omise aims to create an electronic wallet to allow individuals within these countries that have no access to electronic transactions or/and are unbanked. This will give individuals the power to do transactions peer-to-peer.

As you can see, there are several different cryptocurrencies out there with different goals and ideologies. Throughout this book, you'll see that I reinstate the importance of knowing what you're investing in and doing your own research before throwing money in. Quite often than not, beginners will throw in money and follow the hype, and in future chapters, I'll explain to you why that's the road to losing everything... Furthermore, that being said don't trust this book. This book is a guide based on my own experience. Anything I say is not financial advice, so use this information with your own understanding.

If you're finding this book helpful, please leave an honest review on Amazon. Thank you.

Chapter Three: Benefits and Risks of Investing

Benefits

Financial Self-Determinism and Control

The cryptocurrency networks are one of a kind because they are a digital store of value where people can securely save cryptocurrency units and enter into transactions without the need to rely on any third party regulatory body. After you have acquired and safely secured your cryptocurrency units, it is almost impossible for other people (thieves, hackers, banks or even the government) to take them away from you. The government cannot authorize the freezing of your cryptocurrency account nor stop you from entering into any transactions within the cryptocurrency network. This is the primary reason why people love cryptocurrencies, because the lack of regulation allows free movement of money. The government can only do as much as track cryptocurrency purchases with fiat currencies but they cannot track purchases using cryptocurrencies by the individual.

Lower Cost of Transactions

While frozen accounts may be problematic, you also need to be aware of the cost of getting a transaction ready for use. On top of the unexpected risks of frozen accounts and massive chargebacks when you use payment processors, you will also be exposed to well-known high transaction charges for the services of these payment processors. This can considerably reduce the income of your business.

The transaction charges of PayPal, Google Checkout and Amazon Checkout all begin at 2.9 percent plus $ 0.30 for each transaction. You can enjoy a lower rate of 1.9 percent only if your total transactions for the month amount to more than $ 30,000. Because of this, these exorbitant fees may burden a business with a low-profit margin. The same goes for businesses that require a lot of smaller transactions or those whose products are sold at a nominal price.

In contrast to current day transactions, cryptocurrencies are known for their low fees, a major reason why banks are looking to adopt them. The fees vary according to which cryptocurrency is being traded. Bitcoin is known for their high fees relative to other cryptocurrencies; however, Ethereum and Litecoin can have fees less than 1%. And then there is Ripple... It is basically free (not free but it's really cheap) to send Ripple tokens around. This is important because even though 1-2% may not seem like a lot, but when compounded interest is taken place over months, and years, this could equate to thousands, and even millions on large scale trading. This is true primarily for large banks where billions of dollars' worth of transactions is done annually! To put that into perspective, 2% of 1 billion dollars is $20 million! If you could invest that $20 million into somewhere and got a 10% return, that difference in fees is actually much more than 2%.

It Works Around the World

The cryptocurrency network is considered to be an intrinsically wide-reaching and global network. One of the biggest arguments for cryptocurrencies is the fast and low-cost transaction speeds across the world. You will not have to pass through artificial barriers to make payments to vendors who are based in other countries or regions. In fact, it is not entirely possible to validate where a particular cryptocurrency transaction originated. An online vendor who accepts cryptocurrency units as a mode of payment can instantly gain access to a global market while facing the risk of non-payment from customers who reside outside his own country and who are not bound by the legal system of his government. For example, this will allow individuals from the United States to send money to people in Australia in less than 10 minutes, making this much more convenient than third party transactions which are costly. I tried sending money through Western Union and they charged me around 1.5% on top of a poor exchange rate. With cryptocurrencies, I can send some Litecoin in less than 5 minutes and it'll cost around 20 cents.

You should be aware of whether cryptocurrency use in your area is valid and viable for use. The legality of cryptocurrencies will vary based on the country you get your transaction in. In 2017, the cryptocurrency world saw a larger adoption in cryptocurrency use and cryptocurrency technology. In fact, more Bitcoin ATMs are available, allowing withdrawal of Bitcoin to cash, as well as, more vendors accepting Bitcoin and other cryptocurrencies as a form of payments. These signs show the availability and potential of cryptocurrencies. That being said, there are also countries that are closing off cryptocurrencies.

Risks

Volatility of Cryptocurrency Prices

When someone asks you what the value of the cryptocurrency units that you own is, how can you readily answer the question? The fundamental value of any particular currency is a function of the consumer demand for that currency and the consumers' capability to use the currency to trade it for valuable goods and services. Because a lot of conventional currencies are no longer linked to the worth of an underlying product or commodity such as gold and other precious metals, a cryptocurrency unit will only be valuable when some people or consumers want to own them and use them for trade. So if one day the world decides there is no longer a need for cryptocurrencies, the prices will plummet. Though this is unlikely, it is still a potential risk.

Currently, there are plenty (approximately 7000) of public exchanges that have been set up to allow consumers to buy and sell cryptocurrency units in exchange for dollars or other common currencies. This aids in establishing a fundamental relative value for cryptocurrencies, which then allow vendors to convert their cryptocurrency holdings into other common currencies on a more regular basis. This minimizes the vendors' risk exposure to the price volatility of cryptocurrencies. As more individuals trade cryptocurrencies, the likely hood of cryptocurrencies to become more adopted increases.

Even though during the recent years, the price of cryptocurrencies has significantly fluctuated, there now exist methods that vendors can use to quote cryptocurrency prices relative to their equivalent value in dollar or other common currency. This also allows them to convert the cryptocurrencies they have collected into another currency immediately. A common database for cryptocurrency prices is www.coinmarketcap.com, which shows all cryptocurrencies available on the market, all historical prices, all exchanges with everything you need to know.

This comparatively small market limitation together with the absence of a regulatory body may expose the prices of cryptocurrencies to become manipulated by the market players. It's like what you would expect out of penny stocks and other items that are not as commonplace; it only takes one or two transactions for the values of certain items to be jacked up and artificially influenced. In the past, when there has been positive news, or speculation, some institutions (even countries) can jack up the prices. This has been seen frequently with the Korean market, jacking up various cryptocurrencies such as Ethereum, Ripple and Litecoin (amongst many), resulting in periods where 50% of trade occurs solely in the Korean market.

Several important speculations are being made in various online forums on who may be behind the price manipulation of cryptocurrencies and to what extent. It is quite common to hear cryptocurrency speculators refer to "The Manipulator" when they discuss significant market movements.

"The Manipulator" refers to an unidentified individual or group of people that are assumed to be controlling the cryptocurrency prices through their vast wealth. But it is not clear as to who these people are.

There are various social media channels and networks such as Facebook groups, Youtube channels and other sites such as Reddit, that contain a lot of hype by individuals with extensive influence. Keep in mind, even though they might have a rational reason for their 'hyping' of a specified coin, this could also be considered as market manipulation. My advice is not to take my advice, but also do your own research. There are plenty of individuals that are invested in specific coins that only want to make money. Know what you're investing in. Period.

One thing is for certain that the relatively anonymous nature of cryptocurrencies is a huge part of what allows people to adjust the values of cryptocurrencies as they see fit. This makes for an added risk to the cryptocurrency. Of course, whoever is regulating it could always stop doing so and focus on some other kind of investment in the future, but it can be near impossible to figure out what's going to happen.

Risk of Loss

When you own cryptocurrency units, it is quite apparent that you have the responsibility to ensure that your digital wallet is secured from any potential hazards of loss and theft. This task or responsibility can be quite taxing, especially if you own a substantial number of cryptocurrencies because you will have to use certain tools such as protected encryption, password management and information backup to make sure that your risks are maintained at a low-level.

Several high-profile incidents have already been reported where people made errors and mistakes in handling their cryptocurrency accounts that ultimately led to them losing a large amount of their cryptocurrencies. Since there is no central authority you can approach to seek help or assistance, you may have to completely write off your losses because they may already be unrecoverable.

The risks associated with cryptocurrencies are critical and have to be identified. It should not be a surprise that a virtual currency that is relatively new is in danger of being hacked into. You should be cautious when seeing how this currency is run before you make any trades with it.

Few things to consider...

- Although it may seem common sense, NEVER hand out your private keys to anyone. The private keys given by any wallet is the code that allows direct access to your cryptocurrencies.

- Consider a hardware device. Keeping your funds offline can be added protection, however, the risk of losing your hard-wallet is likely.

- Never leave funds on exchanges. If you've been in the cryptocurrency world for a while, you would know several major hacks in the past that has resulted in multi-million dollar loses. Most notably the Mt. Gox hack.

Additionally, leaving your cryptocurrencies on exchanges leaves your funds subject to the exchanges' rules. A good example is the incident on 1st August 2017, with the introduction of Bitcoin Cash. Any Bitcoin owned on Coinbase, is subject to Coinbase' terms and conditions. Coinbase chose not to give any Bitcoin Cash to any Bitcoin owners during the Bitcoin hardfork. Exchanges are not liable for any loss that has occurred, so protect yourself.

Regulatory Ambiguity

The legal category of cryptocurrencies remains uncertain. Some people consider it as a commodity like gold and silver while other treat it as a viable currency. Still, there are others who look at them as a financial product or something that is legally equal to the gold in World of Warcraft. It is yet to be known if they will someday require licenses and financial rules and regulations for it to become a truly viable currency.

Mt.Gox, which was considered as the biggest Bitcoin exchange market, has reported that they have experienced some difficulties in wiring funds. This is because of certain money laundering investigations done by the government or regulatory agencies.

But cryptocurrencies are intrinsically difficult to regulate because no central authority oversees all transactions. Because of this, it is highly probable that cryptocurrencies can become the primary medium option for people who are into illicit activities such as money laundering and tax evasion.

What makes the cryptocurrency market such a concern is that the protected nature of the currency makes it popular among those who engage in illegal or questionable activities.

But if we stop and think about it, any paper currency such as the US dollar can also have the same risks as described above. It is also possible to complete illegal transactions anonymously using dollar bills because it is possible to exchange it without any auditable paper trails. But the complexity of the cryptocurrency network technology may instigate regulators to see it as a hazard to the rules of law.

Chapter Four: Expert Secrets

It is possible to compare the growth in cryptocurrency technology to the internet boom in the late 1990s. However, some think it could be more. During 2016, the market capitalization of the total cryptocurrency increased by more than 50% in about six months. During the first half of 2017, most cryptocurrencies grew more than 1000%! This seemed unreal, however since its peak in June, the market has found more stability. The statistics on the growth of the top 100 cryptocurrencies are mouth-watering for an investor. To put that into perspective, an average investor within the stock market will receive 8%... a little underwhelming relative to cryptocurrencies. With that in mind, though there have been many who've profited on cryptocurrencies, many individuals have also loss money due to the large fluctuations in the market.

Often there are more to these cryptocurrency projects than the transfer of digital currency, some of them add to or supplant existing processes with much better results. In the years to come, there will be a huge number of conventional and outmoded models, which will be replaced by cryptocurrency-based methods. Investors who are wise will try and decide those cryptocurrency projects that satisfy a real need, and those which are nothing more than fads. If you want to invest in cryptocurrencies, here are five expert secrets that will help you out:

Safeguard against Threats

Anything in the world of technology can be hacked into if plenty of effort is made and cryptocurrencies are no exception to this. One such example comes from how hackers stole about $ 1.2 million in Bitcoins from Inputs.io recently. This came as a result of hacking software designed to find information on the ownership status of Bitcoins. This allowed the hackers to steal the money. Another incident was the infamous Mt. Gox hack which saw 850,000 Bitcoins stolen from accounts, a value worth $460,000,000 at the time or $4.25 Billion today!

What makes this worse is that cryptocurrencies are like cash in that they will be gone without any way to easily replace them if they are stolen. What makes this even worse is that it will be hard for anyone to recoup losses if items are stolen. This creates a strong need to ensure that added protection is used when you are investing. Once cryptocurrencies are lost, it is virtually impossible to get them back. So be careful with what you're doing.

To protect yourself from any potential online threats, please consider protecting yourself with the following considerations:

- Consider using an online 'soft' wallet. Online wallets by name, are wallets created by 3rd parties that are based online. They are protected through various codes and set keys that is given to the individual. You can think of them as a cloud storage, much like iCloud, google drive, most soft wallets are free and easy to sign use. I would highly recommend Exodus wallet. It is one I personally use. www.Exodus.io

Again, do your research. This is just my opinion.

- Transfer any cryptocurrencies that are earned to an offline hardware device. Offline hardware wallets are made to protect individuals from digital hackers. If you are very paranoid about the digital world, I would highly recommend a hardware wallet. Keep in mind that these hard wallets are physical, meaning that if it is lost, it is impossible to recover them. So keep them safe. They are much like USB sticks which contain all your cryptocurrencies on a hardware device. One of the most popular hardware wallet is the Ledger Nano S. For more information, visit wonpublications.com/ledger

- Consider getting an encrypted cloud storage service to work on your account. If you're a beginner, I would recommend just sticking to the two recommendations above

If you aren't comfortable about this, then you can always exchange your cryptocurrencies for cash. You can do this online through any exchange or through different cryptocurrency ATMs depending on where you live and what is available for when you take care of the transaction.

Invest in Cryptocurrencies with Longevity

There are numerous rules you should obey when investing, with some of greater importance than others. The first is the rule of longevity. In highly volatile markets, investing long term allows you to hedge against short term fluctuations. This allows you as an investor to reduce risks. Within the cryptocurrency market, it is very volatile, and depending on the type of investor you are, you can profit on this, however, you can also lose a lot. It is highly recommended to look at the long-term prospects. When selecting a long-term investment, you must choose projects that have this; you must examine not only the product but also those who produced it. You must understand what it is you're investing in and ask: is this service going to be needed or utilized in the years ahead? Is there any competition that will easily outdo this project? Do the developers show commitment? Until you understand what you are truly investing in, there is a lot of risk involved. The multi billionaire Warren Buffet once said

"Never invest in a business you cannot understand."

I cannot stress this statement enough. If you don't believe in the project, you will participate in what I call an emotional rollercoaster. Within cryptocurrencies there are a lot of up and down swings in prices. If you know what you're investing in, and you BELIEVE in the project, you won't stress when prices are going down, in fact, if you're like me, you'll get excited when prices are going down so you can buy more at a sale!

So, these are the three things you need to focus on to determine if a project is worth considering or not:

- A current or developing demand for it – For a project to be valuable there has to be a market value. This is determined by the demand of the project. It doesn't matter if you think it's amazing, if no one else does, it has no real value. Consider looking at cryptocurrencies in the top 10 market capitalization when first starting out. There are a lot of fascinating projects. Visit, www.coinmarketcap.com.

- No serious competition – Any serious competition will reduce the potential growth of the project. There are a lot of cryptocurrencies with the same ideas, this lack of innovation will lead to competition eating each other away.

- Developers with commitment – When investing in anything, whether companies, cryptocurrencies, or stocks, it's important to know who is in charge of operations. Strong leaders will see the company progress faster. A good example is Elon Musk of Tesla and SpaceX, as well as Steve Jobs of Apple. Within cryptocurrency, a good example is Vitalik Buterin, the founder of Ethereum, or Charlie Lee of Litecoin.

Focus on Platform, not just Features

This is very important, as a lot of the current cryptocurrency projects are merely full of features, but don't offer a platform of significance. You may well ask what on Earth is meant by a platform. By platform, we mean a cryptocurrency that has a number of different services. In other words, it does or facilitates something apart from being electronic money. Some cryptocurrencies are geared to a particular market such as betting or legalizing marijuana.

Today there are only 20 to 30 viable cryptocurrency projects, meaning the remaining hundreds are of little use as investments with long-term prospects. Cryptocurrencies such as Bitcoin or Ethereum, with tremendous momentum and support, are platforms.

In assessing a cryptocurrency, compare it to the large cryptocurrency platforms like Bitcoin or Ethereum. Ask yourself does the project compare favorably? Is the project well established and does it have a reputation? If it does not, then probably it is not a good long-term investment.

The long term prices of cryptocurrencies are determined by the potential of the projects. So small scale projects have less potential, thus will less likely increase in value over time.

Understand Fees

In the previous chapter we run through the importance of fees. It cannot be emphasized enough how important it is to find exchanges with low fees. Every percentage does matter, and if you're looking to invest regularly, this should be the number one advice you should take. The difference between a 1% and 3% in fees can equate to a 50% reduction in return on investment over extended periods of time. This is due to the nature of *compounding interest*. Some exchanges are made easy for your convenience. They make it easy for new users to understand and use, but this comes at a cost. One popular exchange is Coinbase. Though Coinbase is very simple to use, they have one of the highest fees at around 3.99%. If you must get your cryptocurrency now, it is made for convenience. However, it is not recommended as there are many exchanges with less than 1% fees. Don't be afraid to look around for cheaper exchanges and educate yourself on how to use them. Keep in mind some exchanges lower the prices of the cryptocurrency but it cost more after fees are implemented. For example,

Coinbase: BTC/USD: $3500 + Fees: 3.99% = $3639.65

Other exchanges: BTC/USD: $3550 + Fees: 0.99% = $3585.145

As you can see on the example, other exchanges have a market price of $3550 on the BTC/USD exchange, a $50 higher valuation than Coinbase. Keep in mind that those fees play a huge role. With fees implemented, Coinbase comes out at just over $50 higher! One thing you should also consider is the opportunity cost involved. That difference of $50 can be reinvested thus the potential gains from reinvestment is also lost when investing in Coinbase.

Don't make Emotional Decisions

If you want to invest, you should never make emotional decisions, especially in the cryptocurrency market. Firstly, the most common problem people have when investing is the Fear Of Missing Out (FOMO). It is this fear that drives people to make irrational decisions. It drives them to invest more than they can afford, make poor decisions, and overthink. You can see this also as human greed. When the market is blowing up and increasing at 10% per day, people want to get in, it's natural. But understand that the market always punishes greed and rewards the patient. In a highly volatile market such as cryptocurrencies, FOMO is what allows people to lose money. They get in when there is hype, and they run away and panic sell when things are going down. You should remember what your outcome is, your strategy and focus on the long term. The market runs like a roller coaster, and if you can survive the scary slide down, you'll be laughing on your way up. The market always corrects itself, so come in with a strategy, not with emotion.

You should only invest a percentage of your money after doing a lot of research. This percentage is of course very subjective and depends on a number of factors. Although cryptocurrency has a lot of stories where people who only invested a little made fortunes, its volatility means that to get the best results you have to manage your investments. Do not invest more than you can afford to lose, particularly if the whole world of investment is new to you. It is so easy to underestimate the risks posed by this volatility. Experiment with a small sum like $20 until you know what you're doing.

Here is a suggestion:

If you are less than 30 years old, then no more than 30% cryptocurrency, with a good 50% in safe investments (don't hesitate to seek good advice about what is safe)

If you're in the age range 30 – 40 years old, then no more than 20% cryptocurrency and 60% in Traditional Investments

If you're older than 40 years old, then retirement should be a serious consideration, and you should not have more than 10% cryptocurrency, and you should have at least 70% in Traditional Investments

This is subject to many things like the job you have, the amount of experience you have in investing, your home situation, when you propose to retire, etc.

Even inside your cryptocurrency portfolio, you should have different coins; there are plenty to choose from. This process is called 'spreading your risk.' Never forget the old saying about not putting all your eggs in only one basket.

Chapter Five: Strategies for Risk Minimization

Investing is risky in general and investing in cryptocurrencies is a high-risk, high return activity. At present, there is no other category of investment that has a potential as high as the one offered by cryptocurrencies. However, with high rewards, the risk involved is quite high too. As a crypto investor, there are a couple of risks that you should be aware of.

Market risks

Cryptocurrencies and all kinds of digital tokens are considered to be extremely volatile. The volatility of Bitcoins has relatively reduced over the years, but all the other forms of cryptocurrencies experience intra-day price movements that can move in either direction. The market for cryptocurrencies is news-driven, and every crypto has its risk, rumors, sensationalized headlines and spiteful media campaigns by the rival blockchain technologies which can result in significant price drops and unfavorable fluctuations in the value of the cryptocurrencies. As an investor, you can significantly reduce your market risk by diversifying your investment portfolio. Your portfolio of cryptocurrencies shouldn't consist of just one form of crypto and should have smallholdings of other altcoins as well. You can further reduce your market risk by hedging your investment portfolio with BTC futures as well.

Liquidity risk

Another challenge that investors who are investing in mid-cap and small-cap coins is the risk of liquidity. At present, the average trading volume of Bitcoin per day is over $2 billion. If you leave the ten largest cryptos according to their market share, investors are left with a trading volume that's less than $100 million daily, and in most of the cases, it is less than $10 million. Anyone who is looking to make a more significant investment will find this situation quite challenging. Not just that, the trading volumes of the cryptos are spread over different exchanges, and it makes it quite tricky to execute a large order. To mitigate the risk posed by liquidity, try sticking to those cryptos that are quite liquid, especially when you are trading in large volumes.

Regulatory risk

Cryptocurrencies are a decentralized form of currencies. However, regulatory uncertainty poses a significant hurdle for any seller. Whenever a considerable cryptocurrency trading platform announces any adverse cryptocurrency norms, the entire market gets shaken. For instance, China has recently proclaimed a ban on ICOs (initial coin offerings), and this caused a significant drop in the prices of Chinese digital currencies like NEO. Regulatory risk isn't just confined to one region of the world. All those who are investing in cryptocurrencies should follow any legal news about the tokens they are investing in quite regularly. At present, the major governments of the world haven't banned the use of cryptocurrencies. However, if they do so, then the effect can be devastating. Sadly, regulatory risk cannot be mitigated, and all that an investor can do is follow the news closely and act in accordance with what they learn.

Operational risk

When it comes to trading cryptocurrencies and storing funds, operational risks are bound to exist. The major centralized Bitcoin exchanges happen to be frequent targets for cybercriminals. Even if you are making use of own wallets to store your funds, you might still suffer a loss if you don't store your holdings in cold storage. If you are interested in minimizing the operational risk you face, then you should make use of decentralized exchanges and opt for hardware wallets while storing your funds.

Cyber security risk

Regardless of what you would like to believe, if you are investing in cryptocurrencies, you are a target for hackers. Most of the digitized currencies are pseudonymous, and this makes them an ideal target for cybercriminals out there. Unfortunately, the crypto space is filled with fake websites, fraudulent email campaigns, and targeted hacking of vulnerable trading platforms. A significant risk that crypto investors should be aware of is cybercrime. There are no generalized tips for mitigating this risk and, as an investor, you should take all the necessary steps to ensure the cyber-safety of your investments and holdings.

Fraud risk

Numerous schemes promise unrealistically high returns and are often promoted across different social media platforms and at times are even advertised on reputable cryptocurrency media outlets. Usually, these are just pyramid schemes. However, scammers keep coming up with fraudulent ICOs to scam novice investors. Prudence and research can prevent you from falling prey to such scams. Make sure that you are doing your research and aren't investing because someone asked or told you to.

Well, it might seem like there are plenty of risks that you might have to face as an investor, but you can successfully mitigate your chances by taking a couple of simple steps. Make sure that you keep these risks in mind before entering the cryptocurrency market.

Chapter Six: Tips for trading

Cryptocurrencies are also known as virtual currencies, and their share in the fiscal economy is rapidly increasing. As of now, there are more than 800 cryptocurrencies. Investing in cryptos isn't an exact rocket science. Unlike a company that publicly trades its stocks, there are no financial statements to go through or compare and therefore it is impossible to calculate their book value. Since the intrinsic value of cryptos isn't known, it is difficult to determine whether they have been undervalued or not.

A simple trading fact that you should accept is that you will never be able to time your buys or sells correctly in the crypto space. Selling isn't an exact science and, therefore, there isn't one single strategy that you can follow to acquire more wealth. Every trader has different goals, and all cryptocurrencies are different. No two traders or currencies are alike. In this section, you will learn about some tips that you can make use of while investing in cryptocurrencies.

Understanding the power of cryptocurrencies

People tend to think that investing in cryptocurrencies is the same as investing in stocks. Well, cryptocurrencies aren't stocks, and they aren't commodities. Cryptocurrencies have prices but are entirely different from stocks fundamentally. The process of exchange might be similar. The underlying technology that powers different cryptos can be potentially adapted for retail and institutional capital. The decentralized nature of the digitized currencies means that there isn't much scope for their manipulation. You should invest in cryptos because that's the future of investments and you should believe in it as well.

Select a strategy

How often do you want to buy or sell? Do you want to be a day trader, or do you want to hold on to your cryptos for a while? The general rule of thumb is that the longer you hold your digitized tokens for, the less is the risk you can incur. The same rule of investing that applies to stocks applies to cryptocurrencies as well. However, this doesn't mean that when the circumstances aren't favorable, you hold on to them. Learn to cut your losses and exit when it seems like you are losing in the market. Structural issues are an indicator of failure and learn to recognize such signs.

The initial investment

Dollar cost averaging your purchases of cryptocurrencies will help in reducing the risk of any sudden changes. This will help to reduce the prick of any sudden price fluctuations the tokens might experience in the market. Stick to your gut when it comes to investing, but this doesn't mean that you ignore the market trends.

Hedging your bets

Several exchanges allow you short orders as well. It allows you to place a bet on either side of the price movements of your cryptocurrencies. For instance, a simple strategy would be to put 90% on long and the rest on short orders. This approach means that you are confident about the extended position and it can be made use of for any level of risk.

Trading in altcoins

Bitcoins and other established cryptocurrencies might seem quite tempting. But the world of digitized currencies isn't restricted to just the popular cryptos. So, don't ignore other altcoins. The smaller market capitalization they offer means that they are prone to higher movements in their price. Different altcoins are created to cater to different needs and niches. The risk of investing in altcoins might be high, but then so are the returns. You can allocate specific percentages to different altcoins depending on your tolerance of risk. It is quite similar to managing a fund. Some altcoins are more stable than Ethereum, but others can be very volatile. So, a significant chunk of your portfolio can consist of the famous cryptocurrencies, and the rest can be made up of other altcoins.

Get into the game

Bitcoins are at an all-time high, and the returns they are offering are quite high as well. All the tips and information you have gathered so far will be of no use if you don't get into the game.

You should get started with investing. After all, gaining experience is the best way to learn. Start with a small investment, and you can slowly progress towards more significant investments.

Separate wallets

Never use a single portfolio for storing all your cryptocurrencies. If you are using one wallet for spending and storing your cryptos, you are making yourself vulnerable to cyber threats and attacks. You can create as many Bitcoin addresses as you want. So, it makes sense to make use of different wallets for this purpose. Use different addresses for storing, sending, and receiving cryptocurrencies.

Web wallets shouldn't be used for safekeeping

Web wallets are easy to use. However, it doesn't necessarily mean that they are secure as well. In fact, you are making yourself a soft target for all the potential hackers. If someone manages to hack into your web wallet, you might as well forget about your precious coins. You can make use of a web wallet to hold onto small savings and quick transactions, but that's about it. Always store your savings on a hardware wallet that isn't online. Cryptos don't work for your credit or debit cards. Once your card gets stolen, you lose it or even forget the password; you have the option of blocking and receiving a new one. However, you cannot do this with cryptocurrencies. Since the network is based on anonymity and it is decentralized, there isn't a regulatory authority that you can report the theft too, and you are bound to lose your coins. So, be careful with your tokens.

Protecting your privacy

You are the only one who is responsible for your security and no one else. You wouldn't share the PIN of your bank account with others, would you? Similarly, you shouldn't share your private key with anyone else. The wallet address you use is like your bank account, and your key is like the PIN. The private key is necessary to officiate a transaction. Anyone who is in possession of your private key and the wallet address can easily siphon the funds from your account. Let us keep all the technical aspects aside for a moment. Isn't it foolish to divulge your private information to a stranger?

Cold storage

You are vulnerable, even if your cryptocurrency is stored in a wallet on your computer. Applications of different wallets tend to store user data, and its location can be predicted easily. It is a severe breach of security if someone can access all your financial information. A simple solution is to store your private key on an offline media. Ensuring additional safety will do you no harm, and it will help in securing your hard-earned money. You have the option of printing the private key on a piece of paper or even store it on a USB. You can scan your QR code and save it.

Another option is the encryption of your key. Without the code to decrypt it, the numbers of the key would be useless.

Back it up

Now that you have secured your cryptocurrencies from others, the next step is to protect it from yourself. Yes, you need to protect it from yourself as well. Always make it a point to back up your wallet. Scan your private key and store it in a couple of places. Make multiple copies so that even if one copy is lost, you can still retrieve your secret key without worrying about preceding your investment.

Never invest more than you can afford to lose

When it comes to investing in any form of security, it is essential that you spend wisely. You should never invest more than the loss you can afford. Cryptos are volatile and speculative. The chances of earning a profit or incurring a loss are equally high. So, if you are taking a risk, make sure that it is a calculated one and not an impulsive one. One poor decision can lead to a significant loss. You should be comfortable with the investment that you are making. Always prepare for the worst, you never know what might happen to your investment. You might even end up losing everything. Also, try and diversify your portfolio so that you don't miss everything due to the volatility of a single cryptocurrency.

Set goals for every trade you make

It is quintessential that you have set goals for every deal that you think of making. It will help to keep a steady mind even when the market conditions aren't favorable. Set a price limit at which you should take profits and cut your losses. Set these two limits before you think about entering the market. This will help you in staying level headed without getting swayed by emotions.

Technology

If you are thinking about investing in a programmable currency then you will need a basic understanding of the underlying technology. Most cryptocurrencies make use of the same code as that of a Bitcoin and are just pale copies of the former. Therefore, the investor tends to take little interest in it, unless the Bitcoin fails, as another cryptocurrency can act as its substitute. Take into consideration the validation system that the blockchain makes use of. Does the cryptocurrency make the method of proof of work or evidence of stake? Both are being used simultaneously, or neither is being used. Does it use any other algorithm to check the transactions on the blockchain? What's the governance that's involved, if any? What method of scalability is considered? Is the cryptocurrency even making use of a blockchain? Cryptocurrencies that don't possess the same characteristics as the Bitcoin or the ones that don't use the same language for programming should be studied carefully. Don't assume that all the cryptocurrencies are the same.

The number of tokens created

As an investor, you will be buying tokens, so you should check if the cryptocurrency has a finite number of tokens and if the system is deflationary. The quantum of coins in existence can increase or decrease the price of the cryptocurrency at any point in time. For instance, Bitcoin and Bitcoin cash can only have 21 million tokens at any point in time. So, this is a scarce resource, and with an increase in their demand, their value is bound to increase as well.

The price of a token

Finding a virtual currency that seems to be promising isn't sufficient, you should also know when to buy it. A cryptocurrency can be purchased before its official launch by participating in an ICO or Initial Coin Offering. However, you need to take into consideration the fact that the price of the currency can drop significantly after the brief high of an ICO. If you have missed the ICO, then don't worry. Just wait until the public attention fades away. The price of a cryptocurrency is bound to increase when it is added to an existing trading platform, is taken up by a famous wallet service or when it has reached the stage of track record. It is wise to buy these tokens before the happening of any of these events when the price isn't too high, and you still have a safety margin working in your favor. There are different trading platforms, websites, and exchanges that will provide you with the necessary charts for judging the performance of a cryptocurrency.

Website matters

Check whether the cryptocurrency you want to invest in has an official website of its own. Is there any information available about its creators or the company that's running the operations? Are there any developers and, if yes, then are there biographies and any white papers describing the nature of the cryptocurrency in question? If you cannot find all this information, then it is better if you stay away from such currency. What if it turns out to be a Ponzi scam? Don't invest blindly.

Slack

Slack is the communication platform used by most of the cryptocurrency developers. By registering yourself on slack, you can obtain all the necessary information about the performance of the cryptocurrencies and any advancement made in this regard. Always take into consideration the developers who are responsible for the creation of a particular token. So, do plenty of research, read about the team, and acquire all the information needed and only then should you make a decision about investing. Being prudent is quintessential.

Mistakes to avoid

There are a couple of errors that you should avoid if you want to invest in cryptocurrencies successfully. The first thing that you should do is store your crypto offline. Security should be your priority, and you should always secure your digitized currencies.

Once they are lost, they cannot be recovered. Take precautions while storing your cryptos and store them offline. Don't forget that if you don't have your private key, you cannot access your coins. Do not get carried away by any pump and dump groups. Don't follow these teams and don't think of a quick buy. Instead, do your research and invest in coins sensibly. When in doubt, invest in the popular coins before you think about the obscure ones. Most people tend to buy or spend in certain cryptos because they are considered to be a hot investment at present. However, don't do this. Investing in a crypto that you know nothing about will do you no good. So, take some time and do plenty of research before jumping into the market. Who wouldn't want to make a quick buck? ICOs tend to promote this, but that doesn't mean they are an excellent investing option. Like with any other form of investment, you should do plenty of research on your own before investing in an ICO. After all, it is your hard-earned money that you are thinking about investing. So, that is the least you can do. Don't panic and sell your position. You will end up regretting it. Don't let your emotions guide you when you are engaging in a trade. Be practical and only take calculated risks. Never seek advice from a stranger. Do your research and trust your channels. Make a decision just after gaining a thorough understanding of the crypto you have opted for.

Chapter Seven: All about Bitcoins

Origin of Bitcoin

Satoshi Nakamoto created Bitcoins, and his aim for creating this cryptocurrency was to provide a solution for all the problems that the fiat currency system suffers. In a world where unstable fiat currencies rule the roost, Bitcoins are a refreshing change. The central bank along with other governmental authorities are responsible for devaluating currencies to make goods and services offered seem cheaper in the international market. Devaluation of currencies is also a standard tool used for fighting against inflation. All the price fluctuations in the value of currencies have forced the general public to bear the brunt of booms and fiscal deficits. These reasons led to the conceptualization of a decentralized form of currency. With Bitcoins, the control of the financial system shifts into the hands of the public and its users instead of governmental authorities. Bitcoins are created by using an open source, and it means that anyone can access the platform, make the required improvements, and incorporate new platforms for integration to the existing one. The modern banking systems are capable of integrating the blockchain technology into their existing network of banking. Bitcoins have great potential and have managed to revolutionize the financial system we have been used to. It is an excellent alternative to the conventional method of fiat currencies. There is a constant interaction between the technological and the financial aspects of the world and Bitcoins helps to merge these worlds. The system developed by Nakamoto helps in efficiently getting rid of all middlemen involved in the commercial world. The Bitcoin ecosystem is made up of just the users, and that means that if there aren't any users, these coins will cease to exist altogether.

The more significant is the number of users, the more efficient and effective this system will be. The Bitcoin network depends and belongs to the users and no one else. It is based on the simple concept of peer-to-peer sharing. It implies that whenever a transaction takes place, the two parties involved in it are the buyer and the sender and that's about it. For instance, if A is transferring Bitcoins to B, then A and B are the only parties involved. All the users and anyone who decides to make use of these tokens can easily access a monetary system like this one.

History of Bitcoins

Satoshi Nakamoto published the white paper on Bitcoins that led to their conceptualization. The white paper was titled as "Bitcoin: A Peer-to-Peer Electronic Cash System." All the information along with the different uses this system can be put to was explained in great detail in this paper. The Bitcoin network came into existence sometime during 2009, and the first open source code client along with the first Bitcoin was issued. Nakamoto generated the first block of Bitcoins and, as a reward, he received 50 Bitcoins. Hal Finney and Nakamoto were the two parties amongst whom the first ever Bitcoin transaction took place. Finney downloaded the Bitcoin client, and he received ten Bitcoins for doing so. By 2011, Bitcoins started gaining momentum. Vitalik Buterin began the first magazine on Bitcoins in 2011 and started promoting the concept of cryptocurrencies. In the year 2017, Bitcoins became more expensive than an ounce of gold! Well, that is something, isn't it?

What is a Bitcoin?

Now that you know the story of how Bitcoins were conceptualized, the next thing you should understand is what a Bitcoin is. Bitcoin is a form of digitized currency, and it is based on a long code that can be circulated on the net and is governed by the users who are known as miners. It is self-contained, and it is a virtual currency. Therefore, it effectively eliminates the need to depend on a third party like a bank for its storage, safekeeping and transacting. Once you have its ownership, it is like holding onto bullion or gold that can be used for purchasing things. People hold onto these coins in the hope that their value will increase and well, it indeed has grown exponentially.

Bitcoins are traded from wallet to another on the Internet. A Bitcoin wallet is a private database that can store your coins online or offline. Bitcoins are quite secure, and they indeed cannot be forged like the fiat currencies we use. The computational effort required forging a single Bitcoin makes the process redundant. Just like any other form of money, the value of a Bitcoin keeps fluctuating too. You can make use of different websites like Coindesk for tracking and checking the process of

Bitcoins. The Bitcoin protocol was designed in such a way that only a finite number of coins can exist. The cap on the number of Bitcoins available makes them all the more valuable. The demand for these coins can increase, but there won't be a corresponding increase in the supply. The combined value of all the Bitcoins being traded currently is more than $2 billion. Since this network is entirely decentralized, there is no scope for intervention by regulatory bodies or governmental agencies alike. Miners are users of Bitcoins, and they are scattered all over the world. Miners and their devoted networks help in securing the Bitcoin blockchain and for verifying every transaction that ever takes place. In return for all the efforts they put in, for every block they mine, they get awarded a fixed number of Bitcoins. Every transaction that takes place needs to be verified by multiple users located all over the world, and this minimizes the scope for any fraud or discrepancies. If there is a discrepancy in a single transaction, the code of the entire blockchain changes and it can be spotted right away.

Who created Bitcoins?

Satoshi Nakamoto proposed the idea of digitized currency named Bitcoins. It is mostly a form of electronic payments that are based on mathematical equations or code. The premise was to develop a type of money that's free from the dependency on regulatory bodies or authorities. They can be exchanged quite easily and quickly.

Can they be printed?

Bitcoins aren't governed by any regulatory body, and they exist in digitized form. Therefore, they aren't capable of being printed, and it altogether eliminates the need for a printed copy. Governments or any other central regulatory authorities can write as many notes as they want to, to meet the financial needs of an economy. However, this cannot be done with Bitcoins. When the Bitcoin technology was conceptualized, a cap on the number of Bitcoins that can exist was established as well. It is based on a digitized network that is distributed all over the world. Once the Bitcoin limit has been reached, further Bitcoins cannot be created.

What is a Bitcoin-based on?

The fiat currency system that is in existence is backed by some form of precious metal. So, any fiat currency you own can, in theory, be exchanged for its value in the precious metal that is backing it. However, this doesn't work for Bitcoins. The Bitcoin ecosystem came into existence because of its users and no one else. It is supported by lengthy mathematical equations and functions because of dedicated software. The specialized software used by miners helps in mining blocks of data that in turn helps in unearthing Bitcoins. The software used is an open source code, and anyone can download it and start using it.

Bitcoin consists of different data files that are collectively referred to as the blockchain. Every blockchain has three portions. The first two help in classifying the address and recording the history of any transaction or trades conducted with Bitcoins. It fundamentally makes up the ledger section of Bitcoins. The third portion of the blockchain includes a crucial private header log. The header is an intricate part of the Bitcoin technology and is used for confirming and authorizing a transaction by recording the digital signature used. Every signature is unique, and it is related to the wallet that it's been linked with.

The security system of this crypto consists of different digital names that are capable of being tracked and traced on the Internet since it is a part of the information of the blockchain that's available for public viewing. All these files are anonymous and don't reveal the identity of the user. Anonymity is maintained since this data is displayed as a sequence of numbers that the Bitcoin wallet is associated with for transacting. The blockchain is designed in such a manner that it doesn't record the identity of the user and the Bitcoins will be present in your secure wallet. Only the accounting information is available in the public ledger on the network. So, it effectively acts a deterrent for any illegal activities.

Characteristics of Bitcoins

Like mentioned earlier, Bitcoin is a digitized form of currency, and it means that no regulatory authority can govern or control it. Every machine on the network is capable of mining and processing the Bitcoin transactions and is a part of a global system. All the computers or nodes on this network work as one team. In theory, once you own specific Bitcoins, no one has the authority to take these away from you. Nothing can disrupt this process or the network. Do you remember all the procedures that you had to go through for setting up your bank account? It was quite cumbersome and tedious, wasn't it? Well, you no longer have to jump through hoops to set up your cryptocurrency address. In fact, it takes only a couple of minutes, and you are good to go. The Bitcoin network offers anonymity along with security. You can secure your transactions without having to reveal any personal details. Users are even allowed to set up multiple addresses on the Bitcoin network, and none of these addresses are attached to the personal information. Bitcoin ecosystem is entirely transparent in it's functioning, and every transaction that ever took place on the network since its inception is recorded in the lengthy blockchain that backs it. Think of the blockchain as a transactional ledger that anyone can view. Don't worry; others wouldn't be privy to your personal information. Whenever you make use of a third-party service for creating a transaction in fiat currencies, a transaction fee is levied. You don't have to worry about high transactional fees with Bitcoins and even if a payment is chargeable, it is nominal. A transaction on the Bitcoin network cannot be reversed once it has been authorized.

Let's get familiar with Bitcoins

Bitcoins, during the initial phase, were considered to be a disruptive financial force that's well ahead of its time. However, over time, there has been an increase in the portion of the public that is welcoming this futuristic currency. Bitcoin allows the user to transfer funds to anyone anywhere in the world without having to worry about the involvement of intermediaries. Bitcoin was created with the aim of creating a currency that will help in shifting the power of control to the individual dealing with it and not any other regulatory body. Bitcoin isn't a currency in its strict sense of meaning, but it is a method of digitized payment that can be used for acquiring different goods and services online. Existing businesses have the option of conducting their transactions by using cryptocurrency as well as fiat money. The process of setting up a Bitcoin wallet is simple and doesn't need any additional infrastructure. There are no other costs that are involved in accepting payments made in Bitcoins. Once you have Bitcoins in your possession, you can easily convert them into any of the local currencies you want, and the same can be easily transferred to your bank account. Users have the option of purchasing this cryptocurrency directly, or they can use other cryptocurrencies for obtaining the same.

Blockchain technology

The best possible manner in which one can understand the Bitcoin blockchain is by comparing it a transactional ledger that is publicly available. It helps in ensuring transparency in operations by handing the control over the entire system of accounting to the general public. The blockchain helps in recording, compiling, and verifying all the Bitcoin transactions that have and still are taking place since its conceptualization almost a decade ago. Every deal that was ever made has to be checked and only then will it be recorded on the existing blockchain. Since it is present in a decentralized form, there isn't a single point from which the whole network can be razed to the ground. The data is processed and recorded not just by one authority, but also by tens of thousands of users spread all over the world. This distribution of power and information make the network infallible to the threat of hacking or theft.

The blockchain comprises of vast blocks of data that help in recording and verifying every transaction that's ever occurred. The network is always aware of all transactions relating to every single coin ever produced, and every coin is accounted for on it as well. The blockchain is a public ledger that records all the past and present transactions and all the transactions that will take place in the future as well. It is similar to bookkeeping. Bookkeeping is an essential aspect of the functioning of any organization, and this is usually private information. However, when it comes to Bitcoins, this information is public. It doesn't mean that the feature of anonymity is lost. The identity of the user is never divulged. The blockchain just keeps track of all transactions and the transaction when recorded on the blockchain is only recorded in the form of wallet addresses. The identity of the owner is always secure. So, security is ensured while improving transparency.

The blockchain is a public database of all Bitcoin transactions. A Bitcoin node on the network is a computer that is running a wallet application and is used for detecting and validating every new transaction that involves Bitcoins. Every single node on the system will have access to the entire transactional history of Bitcoins. The blockchain network keeps on increasing whenever a new block is added to it after it has been verified and recorded by these nodes. Every new block of data that's added will consist of a summary of the previous block on the network. Once a block has been added to the system, it cannot be altered. In 2013, it was recorded that the blockchain had more than 50Gb data on it.

How to compete for coins?

A miner will seal a block, and all miners compete with each other to do this. There is a particular software that they tend to make use of for mining blocks of data. Every time a miner has generated the hash, such miner will receive 25 Bitcoins as a reward. The blockchain is continuously updated, and whenever it is updated, every miner on the network will get to know about it. The incentive of receiving Bitcoins keeps the miners interested while securing the entire network. A small snag in this is the ease with which a hash can be produced. Computers are good at this. So, to make it slightly more difficult, the Bitcoin protocol was designed in such a way that it makes this process quite tricky by something that's known as "proof of work."

This protocol doesn't accept any old hash that's created, and some criteria have to be fulfilled. The mixture of a block should look in a particular way, and it has to consist a specific number of zeroes in the beginning. There is no possible manner in which it can be determined how a hash has to look until after it has been produced. As and when a new piece of data is added to the mix, the hash will transform too. Miners aren't allowed to interfere with an existing transaction on the block. They should instead change the manner in which the data is being used for creating a hash. They do this by making use of a random piece of data known as a nonce. The nonce is made use of in a transaction for creating its hash. If the hash cannot fit into the given format, then the nonce will have to be changed, and the entire thing needs to be formatted again. It usually takes numerous attempts for finding the perfect nonce that can fit the given requirements and all the miners on the network will keep trying till they find the perfect fit. And once someone obtains the correct hash, all miners will get to know.

The Bitcoin network is a closed ecosystem, and it helps in storing value digitally. People have the option of saving their Bitcoins within their digital wallets and can enter into a transaction without relying on any third parties or regulatory authority. Once you have your Bitcoins with you and you have secured them, then it is virtually impossible for anyone to take these away from you. The government or any other regulatory authority has no power to take them away from you, they cannot freeze your Bitcoin account, and they certainly cannot stop you from transacting over the Bitcoin network. Whenever you are giving your credit or debit card to a vendor or even a merchant, then you are automatically giving them access to your credit line, regardless of the amount involved in the transaction. All these modes of payment operate on a pull basis and once the payment has been initiated the funds are automatically pulled from your account. Cryptocurrencies function on a push basis, and this means that only the holder of these cryptocurrencies is equipped with sending the exact amount to the merchant and no one else can do this.

Buying Bitcoins

Wallets

The first thing that you will need to do will be to get yourself a wallet for your Bitcoins. After this, you will require a place to store your Bitcoins. In the world of cryptocurrencies, a wallet is made use of for storing your Bitcoins. These wallets are quite similar to a bank account that you might have. Depending on the level of security that you are looking for, different wallets are available. Some are like regular spending accounts that are similar to a regular wallet that you carry with you and then there are others that have got a high level of security.

Bitcoin exchanges

There are plenty of Bitcoin exchanges as well as wallets to choose from. There are proper exchanges for institutional traders, and then there are wallet services that are available for someone who is just testing the waters. Most of the transactions, as well as wallets, will store the digital or fiat currency you hold, just like a traditional bank account would. Exchanges and wallets are an excellent option if you ever want to engage in trading.

One-on-one meeting

You buy Bitcoins from a local seller. Different websites will allow for such transactions like LocalBitcoins. These sites will let you meet up with various traders of Bitcoins, and you can decide whether you want to finalize the trade or not.

Mining Bitcoins

The next method by which you can own Bitcoins would be by mining them. You need a PC and a powerful graphics card to get started with mining your Bitcoins. Specific mining devices are referred to as ASICs. The number of Bitcoins still available is steadily dwindling down as time progresses. It means that mining isn't as cost-effective as it was a year ago. Most people end up spending more on the hardware and electricity than they could ever earn from mining. Mining is usually done in pools these days. It means a couple of miners would get together and pool in their resources for mining Bitcoins and then divide the rewards according to a predetermined ratio.

Chapter Eight: All about Ethereum

The first cryptocurrency created was Bitcoin and only after Bitcoin became a success did the idea of inventing other cryptocurrencies come up. Bitcoin is a type of digital currency, and it doesn't have a tangible form. Bitcoins can be made use of for buying things electronically. Cryptocurrencies are similar to the traditional fiat currency, save that they exist in a digital form and are decentralized. Ethereum aims to function as a decentralized Internet and also as a decentralized app store that will provide support for Dapps along the way.

Ethereum isn't "owned" by anyone, but the network that supports it isn't free. The network makes use of "Ether." Ether is a code that is used to pay for the computational resources necessary to run an application or a program. Ether is quite similar to Bitcoin, and it is a bearer asset. Ether doesn't need a third party to process or approve a transaction. It doesn't operate the way digital currency or the payment system works, and it instead focuses on providing "fuel" that will help in the functioning of Dapps on this network. It might seem slightly complicated; however, it isn't.

Dapps is like an online notebook for deleting, posting or modifying a note and you will have to pay a transaction fee in the form of Ether to make the necessary changes. Therefore, Ether has also been referred to as digital oil. Let us take this analogy a little ahead, then the transaction fees are calculated by the amount of gas required for the action. The transactional cost will depend on the computational power necessary and the time needed to get it up and to run. A transaction that will cost 500 gas will be paid in Ether. Thinking of Ethereum from an economic perspective is entirely open-ended. There is a cap that is set on Bitcoins, whereas no such limit applies to Ether.

In 2014, the users who participated in the crowdfunding campaign purchased about 60 million Ether. Nearly 12 million Ether went towards the Ethereum Foundation that comprises of researchers and developers responsible for keeping the ether network going on. 5 Ethers are allocated to a miner every 12 seconds for verifying a transaction that took place on the system. A maximum of 18 million Ethers can be mined in each year, and a new block is created o the network every 12 seconds.

The popularity of cryptocurrencies surged once again after the price of Ether had risen to over $400. That's a 5000% increase in its value. The wealth that is produced by this ever-expanding industry is difficult to comprehend, especially when it is difficult to see where the value of this currency is originating. In this section, let us take a look at a more in-depth look at what Ethereum is all about and how it fares in comparison to Bitcoin.

The essential features of the Ethereum blockchain network are smart contracts and the Ethereum Virtual Machine. These features are the reason why the Ethereum network is so much more than just a regular system of payment that makes use of digital currency. Contracts that are written in code and are considered to be self-executing are known as Smart Contracts.

Other blockchain technologies are capable of executing a Smart Contract, Ethereum has this feature embedded into his payment system, it allows for immediate transfer of value across the global market this is decentralized with zero-downtime, and there are no middlemen involved in this process.

The Bitcoin was created with the intention of being used for the transfer of monetary value. According to the creators of Ethereum, it merely acts as the "gas or fuel" for Smart Contracts. Ethereum can be made use of as a tool of accumulation and transmission of value (it does this with faster transactions than the ones that are offered by the blockchain network of Bitcoins). However, the ETH was intended not just for this but also for providing some functionality to the Smart Contracts, and it can be compared to the transaction fees or the commission charge that banks levy while facilitating a contract

The Ethereum Virtual Machine also referred to, as EVM is a universal computer. The EVM provides its developers the ability not just to operate but even execute almost any kind of application over this network and decentralizes the system.

If there is an attack, the decentralization and the distribution of information in the form of identical blocks that are secured cryptographically across the whole network help Ethereum in getting rid of all the vulnerable points that most of the servers forming the backbone of the Internet suffer from.

Founded by Vitalik Buterin

In the year 2013 Vitalik Buterin came up with the idea of creating Ethereum while being an active participant in the Bitcoin community. The first white paper he published on Ethereum helped in paving the way for building Ethereum. Along with Dr. Gavin Wood, in the year 2014, he co-founded Ethereum. The formal announcement about Ethereum was made by Buterin in Miami at the North American Bitcoin Conference in 2014 in January. The yellow paper created by Dr. Gavin in April in the same year serves as a technical guide for the same. After this, Ethereum was integrated into various programming languages like Java and Javascript that have improved the performance of the software.

It is available on different platforms

Ether is actively traded on various platforms, and it is not restricted to just one platform. Here are a few platforms that offer different ways for trading ETH. If you are skeptical about risking all your hard-earned money, but you still want a share of the action taking place, then there is a platform that will fit the bill. Trading Game helps you in trading in Ethereum without any additional costs, and it is a free application. So, all that you will need to do would be to start exploring the features of this app. Poloniex is a trading platform that has recorded the highest trading volume. Poloniex holds a considerable portion of the Ether market, and it offers several currency pairs like

ETH/USDT, ETH/BTC, ETC/BTC, and so on. This platform also allows for trading of Ethereum Classic.

Platform

Frontier was the initial version of Ethereum, and it was a beta release that provided the developers with a platform for experimenting and learning before they can get started with the creation of decentralized apps and tools that were based on Ethereum. On 30th July in the year 2015, Frontier was launched. The next version of Ethereum that was released was known as the homestead, and it was published on 14th March in the year 2016 (on Pi Day). It was the first ever production release of Ethereum. This upgrade had plenty of changes made to the protocol and the networking change that allowed for further updates in the network. Two more steps are on their way, and their release date hasn't been confirmed yet. The third phase is known as Metropolis and the fourth one as Serenity.

Ether or ETH holds the second most significant part of the cryptocurrency market, right after Bitcoin. During the first quarter of 2017, the market share of Ether has increased by $7 billion, and its price has risen more than five times. When compared to its performance in 2015, the value of ETH has grown more than 2800% since that year. The volume of trade taking place in Ether has been fluctuating, and it will keep on doing so. Ether has great potential, and this is reflected in its present worth. Ether wasn't an overnight success, it has indeed come a long way since it started and it is bound to go further.

Buying Ethereum

Creating an account on the exchange

Like with any other cryptocurrencies, even Ethereum needs to be purchased and sold online via exchanges dealing in this. There are plenty of trading platforms. The most popular options include Kraken, Bitstamp, Coinbase, and Gemini. Before you can start trading in Ethereum, you will need to select an exchange and then create an account on it.

Verifying the account

A good exchange will need to check your account in multiple ways. You might be required to upload a couple of documents to verify your identity and ensuring that your portfolio clears all the necessary regulations. Verification can take a day or two, and it will depend on how popular and busy the exchange that you have opted for actually is.

Depositing fiat currency

The next step would be to collect fiat currency into the account through your bank or even a wire transfer. It would take a day or two for the money to get clearance.

Start trading

When your account is verified, and money has also been deposited in it, then you can start purchasing or selling in Ether and other cryptocurrencies as well. The interface of each exchange would be different, and you need to have some patience to get all the necessary clearances and to confirm the transactions.

Chapter Nine: Litecoin 101

Just like conventional currency, different types of cryptocurrencies are in existence. Since Bitcoin happens to be the first cryptocurrency, it enjoys more publicity than the rest. Litecoin is the new form of digital currency on the block, and it is poised for dynamic growth. In October 2013, Charles Lee, a former Google engineer, unveiled Litecoin. Litecoin was introduced as the "silver" to the "gold" of Bitcoin. Lee had come up with the idea of Litecoin to fix the problems that Bitcoins posed. Litecoin is amongst the top 5 digital currencies that are present in the market and is considered to be a fierce rival of Bitcoin. Litecoin, like several of its counterparts, functions as an online payment system like PayPal or any banking application. Users can quickly conduct transactions using cryptocurrency. Only instead of using fiat currency like the U.S. dollar, the operation is performed in units of Litecoin.

How is Litecoin made?

A government does not issue Litecoin, like the other cryptocurrencies. The government has singularly been the entity throughout history that has been responsible for minting money. The Federal Reserve doesn't regulate Litecoins, and they aren't invented at a press at the Bureau of Engraving and Printing. A complicated process referred to as mining instead creates Litecoins. This method comprises the processing and verification of several Litecoin transactions. Unlike fiat currency, there is a cap on the number of Litecoins present. There can be no more than 84 million Litecoins in circulation. A block is generated on the Litecoin network in every 2.5 minutes. The block is made up of ledger entries of Litecoin transactions that take place around the world. It is where a Litecoin derives its value. The block of transactions is verified by using mining software and is visible to any miner who wishes to see it. Once a block is confirmed, the next block will enter the chain, and this would contain the record of all the Litecoin transactions ever transacted.

Mining for Litecoin

The incentive offered for extraction is that for every block that is successfully verified, 25 Litecoins are awarded. Initially, the number of Litecoins provided as the reward was 50 and from October 2015, it's been reduced to 25. This process of reduction will keep on recurring until all the 84 million Litecoins are mined. Will an unscrupulous miner change the algorithm of the block and enable double spending? Well, this isn't possible and any attempt made to do so can be spotted immediately by the other miners. The identity of any miner that places such an irregularity is always anonymous. The only way the entire blockchain network can be disrupted would be if a majority of miners agree to process the false transactions, this is practically impossible to achieve.

Mining cryptocurrency at a rate that can be considered to be profitable to the miner would need a lot of processing power and specialized hardware. Your regular laptop isn't designed to be fast enough to complete this task. It is where Litecoins differ from their competitors. Any off-the-shelf computers can mine Litecoins. However, a machine with a more significant processing power can help in increasing the chances of earning some Litecoins.

Investing in Litecoin

Litecoin is a powerful digital currency and with the way that it is progressing, it has a lot of potential. If you are thinking about investing in Litecoin, then now is the time. You can purchase these from any of the exchanges or mine them. More information about both these methods has been provided in the coming chapters.

Like mentioned earlier, Litecoin was developed as an alternative to Bitcoin to address some of its shortcomings. Litecoin is lightweight and is more abundant when compared to Bitcoin. The proof-of-work algorithm used by Litecoin is Scrypt, and this algorithm is almost immune to ASIC mining. You will learn more things about getting started with Litecoins in the coming chapters. Here are a few things that you should take into consideration before buying Litecoin.

This cryptocurrency has become quite popular amongst the speculators in the market after the price surge that the Bitcoin experienced in November 2013. The prices of these cryptocurrencies might move similarly. However, the costs of Litecoin are comparatively lower.

The infrastructure of Litecoin is relatively less developed than that of Bitcoin. It might not be a problem for a seasoned investor, but a novice investor might take a while to figure things out. You can earn Litecoins by mining them by using standard computing equipment. You should always do plenty of research on your own, before investing your hard-earned money, and never take on more risk than that you can shoulder.

Cash for Litecoins or Bitcoins for Litecoins?

Once you have made up your mind about buying Litecoins, you will need to decide whether you will want to buy these in exchange for fiat currency or Bitcoins. The infrastructure of Litecoin isn't as developed as that of Bitcoin. The most straightforward manner in which you can acquire Litecoins would be by buying them with Bitcoins. It is the fastest method, and for most of the users, this is cost effective as well.

If you are holding Bitcoins, then you can make use of these to buy Litecoins from any of the listed exchanges like BTC-e, Kraken, Cryptsy, and other transactions. The process of buying Litecoins is yet to be streamlined. There are about two dozen exchanges that deal in Litecoins and most of them allow for the only Bitcoin to Litecoin transactions or vice versa. Couple of exchanges like Bitfinex, Crypto-Trade, Kraken, and BTC-e sells Litecoins for fiat currency (dollars, euros, and rubles only). However, the availability would depend on your location. For instance, in the UK, the investors have the option of directly buying Litecoins from Bittylicious or BitBargain via a banking transfer. However, this isn't the case in most of the countries.

Litecoin mining

Litecoin uses a proof-of-work algorithm that is entirely different from the one that Bitcoin makes use of. Litecoin uses Scrypt hashing algorithm. This algorithm was designed in such a manner that it would be difficult to execute a large-scale hardware attack because of the large quantities of memory this would require. Litecoin mining is a complicated process, and it goes beyond simply checking the blocks of Litecoin transactions. Most people end up spending more on the hardware and electricity than they could ever earn from mining. Mining is usually done in pools these days. It means a couple of miners would get together and pool in their resources to mine Litecoins and then divide the rewards according to a predetermined ratio.

Buying Litecoin

In this chapter, you will learn about the different ways in which you can buy Litecoins by making use of various payment options. Before you get started with buying Litecoins, you should make sure that you have got a good wallet in which you can store your Litecoins.

Buying with credit or debit card

Coinbase: This is perhaps the easiest manner in which you will be able to buy Litecoins with your credit card. The purchase fee that is charged is up to 3.99% of a given purchase. This platform is available in US, UK, Europe, Singapore and Australia. This same platform can also be made use of for buying Litecoins with a bank account or a bank transfer. This option is available in all the countries mentioned above and Canada as well. Americans can make use of ACH transfer (it'll take about 5 to 7 days), and Europeans can make use of SEPA transfer and the waiting period can range from a day to three days. The fees per transaction are about 1.49%.

Buying Litecoin with cash

There is no right way in which you can buy Litecoins with money. The most popular manner for acquiring Bitcoins instead of cash would be via LocalBitcoins. However, this platform doesn't support Litecoin as of now. The other Bitcoin exchanges that are quite popular are BitQuick and Wall of Coins, and neither of these is Litecoin compatible. It means that you will need first to purchase Bitcoins with cash and then exchange these for Litecoin by making use of the methods mentioned above. The same would apply to Bitcoin ATMs as well. Most of them don't support Litecoin. So, if you are interested in buying Litecoin at a Bitcoin ATM, you will need to purchase Bitcoin and then convert them to Litecoin.

Buying Litecoin with PayPal

Just like buying Litecoin with cash, there is no direct way in which you can buy Litecoin with PayPal. You will have to acquire Bitcoin by making use of PayPal, and once you have received

Bitcoins, you will need to convert them into Litecoin. The process of obtaining Bitcoin with PayPal is quite extensive.

Buying Litecoin with Bitcoin

If you are already in possession of Bitcoins, then it is straightforward to convert these into Litecoins. You will need to find an exchange that deals with LTC/BTC transactions. Most of the trades deal in such transactions because they are quite popular.

Changelly: This is perhaps the fastest method that is available for the conversion of Bitcoin to Litecoin. You will just have to enter the number of Litecoin you will want to buy and provide the Litecoin address. Then this platform does the calculations and will inform you the number of Bitcoins that will be necessary for the exchange and the address to which the Bitcoins should be sent. Once you do this, the LTC will be automatically sent to your wallet after a little while.

Buying Litecoin with Skrill

BiPanda also accepts Skrill payments for acquiring Litecoins. The fee will vary and will be included in your buying price.

Buying Litecoin with Ethereum

2017 has been quite a lucky year for Ethereum, and this cryptocurrency has witnessed a massive surge in its prices. Ethereum holders can trade in their ether for buying Litecoin.

Litecoin has got an excellent rate of liquidity, and it is quite popular among traders, especially in China.

Changelly: This is perhaps the single exchange there is, and it is also a fast way to which you can convert Ethereum into Litecoin. When you are making use of Changelly, you don't have to store your money with the exchange (third-party), and this reduces your exposure to the risk of theft. You will merely have to specify the number of Litecoin you will want to buy, specify the address to which the Litecoin needs to be sent. Changelly will do the calculations and will inform you of the number of Ethereum that would be required for this purchase. They will provide an address to which Ether will need to be sent, and within a while, you will receive a deposit of Litecoin to your wallet. Any other form of altcoin can also be converted to Litecoin by making use of Changelly, and the same procedure is applicable.

Poloniex: This is the most significant exchange of altcoin in the world. There is one major drawback of making use of Poloniex for converting your Ethereum to Litecoin. Poloniex does not directly assist in the conversion of Ethereum to Litecoin. You will first have to turn your Ethereum into Bitcoin and then convert this Bitcoin to Litecoin. ShapeShift is quite similar to Changelly. In fact, this was the first company that had come up with the concept of exchange for holding onto your funds.

The most frequently asked question about the conversion of Ethereum to Litecoin is "Why are there only a few options available?" The primary issue present in all of the crypto markets across the globe is liquidity. As the space increases, the liquidity will also improve. However, as of now, Bitcoin is the only cryptocurrency that enjoys a high rate of liquidity. The other cryptocurrencies will soon follow suit. It is the main reason why most of the options regarding the purchase of Litecoin require Bitcoin and then its conversion or exchange.

Buying Litecoin online

Most of the options that have been mentioned above will allow you to buy Litecoins online. You will have to buy them online if you want to acquire them by making use of your credit card, debit card, bank transfer, or even Skrill. The only option where an online removal isn't possible is when you are trying to buy them with cash.

Conclusion

If you are going to invest in cryptocurrencies, the first thing to focus on is research. You have to make judgments for yourself instead of relying on all the information that you have been given. It is after all your money – make sure that you're investing in something worthwhile. So, always look into the history, future and trade practices of the cryptocurrency before making any decisions.

You should also remember that you don't need to invest in only the famous cryptocurrencies. Everybody knows about Bitcoin, and they all want to get in on it. This means that the returns on Bitcoin might not be as good because even Bitcoin at this point requires a hefty sum of initial investment.

You should focus on the upcoming small players like OmiseGo, Ripple, and Golem. These platforms are highly undervalued considering the potential they have. You can invest in them now at a low price to enjoy the benefits when they blow up.

Thank you for buying this book and if you really found this book helpful, please leave an honest review on Amazon.

All the best!

Mastering Bitcoin: The Ultimate Guide for Beginners to Understanding Bitcoin Technology, Bitcoin Investing, Bitcoin Mining and Other Cryptocurrencies.

Introduction

I want to thank you for choosing and purchasing this book, *'Mastering Bitcoin: The Ultimate Guide for Beginners to Understanding Bitcoin Technology, Bitcoin Investing, Bitcoin Mining and Other Cryptocurrencies."* In this book you'll find everything you need to know about Bitcoin, from the history of Bitcoin, to the nitty gritty side of Bitcoin Mining. This book will be your ultimate guide and something you can refer to now, and also in the future. As a BONUS, not only is this book about the essentials of Bitcoin, information about other Cryptocurrencies will be added for your benefit.

If you're like me, you would've heard about Bitcoin somewhere, possibly from a friend, the news, or even the fact that you just wanted to find new ways to make money. I was all the above. Before I started investing into cryptocurrencies, I invested in traditional stocks and bonds, but I realized that it simply wasn't exciting enough. I heard of Bitcoin every now and then, I read that people have been making hundreds of thousands and even MILLIONS on Bitcoin, but I didn't believe it. It wasn't until my friend told me that he made $2000 profit on a $500 investment on Bitcoin that I was blown away. I know what you might be thinking, this isn't that much right? Keeping in mind, this was when we were 21 and he had only invested in Bitcoin for about a year. Traditional investments such as stocks, only make about 8% per year on average, so to obtain a 400% return on investment was mind blowing. I didn't know what Bitcoin really was or what the functions and practical uses were, but I was curious enough to research it and once I dove right into the world of cryptocurrencies, I realized the absolute potential that Bitcoin and the other altcoins (alternative cryptocurrencies) possesses.

I know you are excited to learn about Bitcoin, and we'll get started in a second. Again, I'd like to thank you for choosing this book. I have comprised everything I know about Bitcoin in my years of experience, and I know you'll enjoy this book. This is the beginning of your cryptocurrency adventure and I hope you're as excited as I am.

At the end of this book, you'll be given a FREE step-by-step course so that you can start investing in cryptocurrencies today!

Let's get started!

Chapter 1: History of Bitcoin

The Creation of Cryptocurrency

So as we know, 'cryptocurrency' is the name given to any digital currencies encrypted through a method known as 'cryptography'. One of the first known descriptions of Cryptocurrency comes from Wei Dai in 1998. Most of these currencies during this time were represented by the computer "bit" size. This is likely why you get names like b-money and Bit Gold in the early works of cryptocurrency. Most of Bitcoin was created before Bitcoin existed, such as the famous Proof of Work concept (which will be covered further on) that Bitcoin is currently famous for is a part of Bit Gold. However, nothing really caught on until Bitcoin was created in 2009.

The Failed Currencies before Bitcoin

Wei Dai created the description of b-money but it is undocumented as to whether it was ever put into action. Bit Gold, on the other hand, was physically created by Nick Szabo but, like b-money, was never put into action either. It is often suspected that Szabo was the creator of Bitcoin due to how similar Bit Gold was to Bitcoin (heck, even the name sounds similar) but Nick always refused to lay claim to the program. 1994 brought the year where the EU started regulating Prepaid Cards and this, unintentionally, killed a lot of ideas that involved cryptocurrency. Shortly after, we received the great gift we called PayPal. PayPal was the first step towards cryptocurrency and as PayPal's became more successful, so did the demand for internet money. Welcome Bitcoin.

The Creation of Bitcoin: Satoshi Nakamoto

In 2009, Bitcoin became the first practicable cryptocurrency, proving that a decentralized currency could exist. This is ironic; given that Bitcoin inventor Satoshi Nakamoto never set out to create a new form of money. He wanted to solve the problem of centralized digital cash and created a peer-to-peer digital cash system. He ended up developing Bitcoin, an entirely unregulated form of currency, which relied upon extensive mathematical computations to validate authenticity. It was with the birth of Bitcoin that cryptocurrency became a reality, forever changing how we do transactions.

In 2008, the Satoshi paper was released and the idea of Bitcoin was released in an academic paper titled "Bitcoin: A Peer to Peer Electronic Cash System". Satoshi, who was an anonymous user on that forum, began to circulate their ideas around. The known release of Bitcoin became popular around 2009. Satoshi Nakamoto released the first version of the Bitcoin software (Version 0.1) on 9th January, 2009. The Bitcoin website was created with its domain name as bitcoin.org. From there on, Satoshi went a step ahead to work in partnership with other software developers to improve the Bitcoin software until around the middle of the year 2010. It was until this time that Satoshi announced his departure and transferred control of the network alert key and code base (source code) of the Bitcoin software to Gavin Andresen.

Andresen stated afterwards that he sought to decentralize the functioning of Bitcoin.

"As soon as Satoshi stepped back and threw the project on my shoulde of the things I did was to decentralize that. So if I get hit by a bus," he "it would be clear that the project would go on".

The idea behind Bitcoin was to create a peer to peer, decentralized system where two individuals can send each other transactions without any authorization. This means that if person A wanted to send person B Bitcoin, they could do it without any governing body, like a bank or an external company such as Western Union. The main aim of creating Bitcoin was to come up with a form of currency that cannot be controlled by businesses or governments in that it allows you to conduct trade without having to reveal your identity or having to pay any additional costs.

Once it landed on the market, the Bitcoin market seemed to slowly crawl at first before exploding in 2014, skyrocketing to a value of $1,000 as a market value for a single BTC. The spike in the prices of Bitcoin varied greatly, particularly in 2017, where the prices surged higher than $10,000 for 1 Bitcoin! As of 15th January 2018, 1 bitcoin is worth $13, 938.

The Problems of Bitcoin

There are a few issues with Bitcoin that do not make themselves apparent very quickly. The first problem is that all transactions have no physical middleman, which means that no government can look at all the transactions currently happening. That's not a problem until you realize that everything that used to be difficult to exchange with paper money become all too easy with Bitcoin. The fact that trade transactions cannot be traced back to you makes it a dream come true for money launderers, terrorists, extortionists, cyber criminals and drug dealers. Essentially, that means you can digitally buy drugs with Bitcoin without government interference and the government can't track what Bitcoin is funding.

There are also concerns that unlike all other investment avenues available, bitcoin and other forms of cryptocurrencies are not regulated by central banks or government entities. There isn't any authority you can approach to air your grievances. For instance, if you purchase something with your credit card and get duped, you could always contact your bank and demand for compensation or solve that issue amicably. But what do you think can happen if you get duped in a bitcoin transaction? Do you think no matter what you do you will get your money back? Herein lies the problem of investing through such unregulated schemes.

The other problem is that Bitcoin is the new Gold Standard because there will only ever be a certain amount of Bitcoins available on the market, which means that Bitcoin value will continue rise until it is near unattainable for everyone. This will only happen if the community retains hoarders. The third problem I see, because there could be far more that I don't know about, is the immediate devaluing of current currencies. What happens when the dollar is no longer the reserve income of the world? Where will the trillions of dollars' worth of debt go? The U.S.A. isn't the only country like this either because you have countries with even bigger debts such as Japan, Lebanon, Greece, and Italy. Let's say that Japan gathers ten million Bitcoins (a rough half of all those that will ever exist). Speculators have said the Bitcoin price could go up to $100,000 a BTC. It wouldn't be difficult for Japan to do this either and that's one trillion dollars just so you know. What happens if Japan sells all of those Bitcoins for the USD? That would be a massive economic shift that everyone would feel because when money leaves the country, it puts that country further into debt with the rest of the world. It must now back that trillion dollars that just left the country. It is only when the country brings in money with sold products that it pays off debt and since BTC is a product, it would effectively shift one trillion dollars' worth of debt from Japan to the U.S.A.

Another problem is that once Bitcoin transactions are completed they cannot be reversed. And this can prove to be a huge problem especially if the whole transaction process later proves to be a sham. Cyber criminals have identified this problem and come up with strategies to make the most of such a situation. They are circulating malware (malicious softwares) around the internet that roam and scan people's hard disks searching for bitcoins. Unfortunately for you, if your computer is not secured from such malware and you happen to posses' unencrypted bitcoins in your hard drive, then you risk losing all of them at once without your consent.

Similarly, because of how the Bitcoin was designed, if anyone were to gain access to your 'private key' (password), then that person not only has access to all your bitcoins he/she has the authorization to spend them in whatever way he/she wishes. Just in the same way a robber comes to steal a stack of money that you keep under your bed; a cyber criminal can steal your digital private key and use it to spend your bitcoins.

Fortunately for bitcoin users, there are various countermeasures that you can take to prevent being on the receiving end of such actions. For example, if you have a sizeable amount of bitcoins in your possession, you are advised to move them all to a 'cold storage' (a flash drive or hard disk that is not connected to any computer connected to the internet and then hidden in a secure location such as a physical safe. Currently, bitcoin developers are still working on a new software patch to address the same problem. They are trying to come up with a technology known as the **multi signature transactions** that will not submit a transaction to the network before two or more people sign and clear it for approval.

Let's take our discussion about bitcoin a bit further.

Chapter 2: Understanding Bitcoin

Bitcoin is digital or virtual money. Created in 2009, bitcoin became the first decentralized digital currency, which works without the control of a central authority e.g., a central bank. The bitcoin network is peer to peer and the transactions that take place within the network take place between individual users without any intermediary. When a transaction is initiated, it is verified by a network of computers (known as nodes) with the use of cryptocurrency after which the transaction is recorded in a public distributed ledger referred to as blockchain. Bitcoins are not like the physical coins you have in your wallet or purse. They are basically coded language, a line of digital 0's and 1's that are used in computer programming. They are however similar to tangible currency in that once you acquire them, you can buy anything with them or exchange them for services or even normal currency.

Fiat Money

A lot of people have a hard time wrapping their head around Bitcoin but the honest truth is that Bitcoin is not that different from our actual physical money. Did you know the World's Reserve Dollar represents the most basic form of a Fiat money? A Fiat money has its value determined by the people rather than by the value of another object. For instance, the U.S. dollar is backed by an estimated value but in the past, it has been backed by the gold standard or, rather, the worth gold stood for (fiat on top of fiat, you could say). The gold standard means that a certain portion of money represents a very specific amount of gold. Many countries start off with the gold standard and move on from it, but many people believe that the gold standard helps control economics and wish to go back to it. The problem with gold is that it simply acts as a middleman for fiat money and so money would do the same thing with or without gold. The only way for money to stabilize, to some, is to simply stop printing more money. However, because it's no longer representing gold as a value and it has a value of its own, this now becomes a Fiat money. Bitcoin is similar in that the value of Bitcoin is set by the market or, rather, how much someone is willing to spend in order to gain access to Bitcoin.

Bitcoin Is Similar To Gold; But Way Better

Bitcoin shares many similarities with gold and one common characteristic they share is that they both have a finite supply. It is not possible to simply pull gold in arbitrary quantities from thin air. You have to mine or extract it from the ground and thereafter supply it into the market for circulation depending on the market prices. The problem with the gold standard is that it actually gets in the way of the banking capability to give out fiduciary media.
Bitcoin therefore has been credited with taking the benefits that gold brings a notch higher, the only difference is that it is digital.
Gold as you know not only takes a lot of physical space but it is also very heavy and that is why if you are under the gold standard, you will prefer to substitute the gold for paper. This system ensures that the gold is left in the banks and you put your faith in the bank that it will handle your gold responsibly. Therefore, even when the strict gold standard becomes more strict, some of these financial institutions are tempted to betray their clients' trust by making new deposits and giving out fiduciary media.
But then the savior in the mould of Bitcoin came along. Since it operates on a digital platform, it takes up no physical space and also costs next to nothing to store unlike its predecessor. As a result, you can carry bitcoin with you anywhere in the world without an extra load.

And better still, you don't even need paper substitutes for your bitcoins and neither will there be any need to give the banks an opportunity to take money from you. And just like you can break down gold into small units for carrying around, bitcoin is even better, as it has its own units, which means anyone who wants to invest in bitcoins can afford it with a lot of ease.

Common Bitcoin Measurement Units

The way you can break down a €100 (a hundred euro) note/bill into 100 €1 coins is the same way you can also break down 1 bitcoin (the currency abbreviated as BTC like USD is for the American dollar) into smaller units. Since the value of the bitcoin is gradually soaring from time to time (as of 15th January 2018, 1 bitcoin is worth $13, 938), the prices of many commodities in the market have to be displayed as an alternative metric system of denomination in fractional bitcoin currency.

For example, the value of one ink pen can be 0.001 BTC. The problem is that such fractional numerical prices can be a bit complicated or confusing to read. To make the reading much easier, we can convert the bitcoin to the **bit** sub unit (1 bit = 0.000001 bitcoins). In this case, the aforementioned pen will cost 1000 bits. You can now see that such use of the fractional bitcoin currencies makes the reading of bitcoin prices much more intuitive and also very memorable.

The main aim of the bitcoin currency (BTC) is to ensure that it forges harmony with the rest of all the other currencies globally. To accomplish this goal therefore, the creators of bitcoin ensured that a single bitcoin could be divisible all the way down to the 8th decimal place. In figures, this translates to 0.00000001 BTC or $1/_{100000000}$ BTC. Likewise, 1 bitcoin is equal to 1 million bits.

The smallest denomination or unit of the bitcoin is the satoshi, which is just but homage that recognizes the founding father of the Bitcoin protocol, Satoshi Nakamoto. the 2nd smallest sub unit is known as the finney. It was also names after Hal Finney, a man who is considered to be one of bitcoin's first pioneers and also made contact with Satoshi.

The table below shows the list of the bitcoin metric system of denominations; all the way from the largest (BTC) to the least in value (satoshi).

#	DENOMINATION	ABBREVIATION	FAMILIAR NAME	VALUE
1	Bitcoin	BTC	Bitcoin	1
2	Decibit	dBTC	Deci-bitcoin	0.1
3	Centibit	cBTC	Centi-bitcoin	0.01
4	Millibit	mBTC	Milli-bitcoin	0.001
5	Bit (Microbit)	µBTC	Bit (Micro-bitcoin)	0.00000
6	Finney	FIN	Finney	0.00000
7	Satoshi	SAT	Satoshi	0.00000

I know you might be wondering; so how do people arrive at the prices that you see on the news? Let's discuss that next.

How Is The Value Of Bitcoin Determined?

The value of 1 bitcoin is largely dependent on the supply and demand theory. In simple terms, the value is determined by fluctuations of the market just as is the case with all other currencies. If the demand for bitcoins increases or if the supply reduces, then the value of a bitcoin increases and the reverse is also true. Nevertheless, the bitcoin was created to always appreciate in terms of value as time elapses. And this is the reason why it has such a big number of denominations. New bitcoins are released into the market at an estimated rate of 1 new coin every 24 seconds. Up to date, there are around 16 million bitcoins circulating since the first ever coins were introduced in the year 2009. The bitcoin system is different from the traditional currencies in that the reserve of bitcoins is fixed. But the supply of bitcoins will eventually stop as this system has been programmed to ensure that only a total of an exact 21 million bitcoins can ever be in circulation.

If this is the case, then calculations show that around the year 2140, all the available 21 million bitcoins will be in circulation and there won't be any free coins left in the store to extract as rewards from mining. By this point, the Bitcoin currency will have appreciated to immeasurable proportions and this is the reason why it was broken down into many sub units. In this respect, if the worth of a solitary bitcoin multiplies by thousands or millions of dollars, then you will still be able to use it to purchase the cheapest commodity available on the internet.

We've mentioned cryptocurrency multiple times in the book. What exactly is cryptocurrency?

Cryptocurrency

Cryptocurrency is refers to the name given to all digital currencies encrypted through cryptography. If you think of all the physical currencies (US dollar, Australian dollar, Japanese Yen, Euro, etc.), what separates these physical currencies from cryptocurrencies is digitization. This means you can't physically hold cryptocurrencies, such as Bitcoin. You can think of Bitcoin as the dollar and other big players like Ethereum and Litecoin as other currencies.

The term 'Cryptocurrency' isn't all that new; it was actually available to us in the 1980s, but only recently have we developed a method to where we can utilize cryptocurrency and validate the worth of the currency. You see, previous cryptocurrencies relied on single transfer computers and this caused an issue known as the double spending problem. In reality, you had no way of proving that the currency that you obtained was lawfully obtained and not just created on your computer via copy and paste. Since most cryptocurrencies were from public sources and could be recreated, we simply couldn't trust cryptocurrency but with Bitcoin, the story changed. Bitcoin works as a peer-to-peer connection in that everyone has a validating key that determines how many Bitcoins are on the market at the time and who has those Bitcoins. If your Bitcoin isn't one of those Bitcoins when it is validated against the system, it is seen as a fake and this provides validity and trustworthiness in the Bitcoin system. You have a public key, which is what you share with everybody else whenever you want to spend or receive Bitcoins and then you have the private key, which is what is used whenever the transaction occurs to validate your Bitcoins. This simplistic process allows for the validation of the Bitcoins and since the top Security Experts in the world have said that such a system is trustworthy, we now recognize Bitcoin as a vetted cryptocurrency.

How Encryption Makes The Use Of Cryptocurrencies Secure

You already know that cryptocurrencies such as Ethereum and Bitcoin use a peer to peer decentralized system to carry out transactions. And given the fact that all this is done online, some concerns were raised that such transactions might be volatile or worse still prone to cyber attacks from hackers. Now you need not worry about any of these because cryptocurrencies use cryptography to ensure that whatever transactions you carry out are secured to the highest degree. Cryptography from an Information technology point of view is associated with the process of securing electronic information in the presence adversaries (of malicious 3rd parties) when communicating. This is done by encryption (converting the readable text into cipher text (text format that is unreadable)). The cipher text can only be reconverted back to readable text only by use of a special secret key and an algorithm. A particular algorithm will always convert the same readable text into cipher text and vice versa if the same key is used. Any algorithm is secure to use for encryption provided that a hacker will be unable to determine the properties of readable text or the key even after obtaining the cipher text.

Problems with Old Cryptocurrency

Cryptocurrency does have a few problems with it due to the fact that there are several inconsistencies that naturally occur with money. The first problem is that there are several different types of cryptocurrencies. As I've already said, we've had the technology since the 1980s. It has only been in recent history that we have had some success with Bitcoin and this means that there are going to be several different types of cryptocurrencies available for you to get. The second problem is an additional effect with having more than one type of currency. Due to the fact that there are several different types of cryptocurrencies, the variation in value constantly changes all the time. This means that sometimes Bitcoin will be the most valued but other times it may be more effective to farm a new type of cryptocurrency.

Another problem is that the processing speed of cryptocurrency transactions like that of bitcoin is usually slow. The slow nature is due to the protection of the blockchains that make such cryptocurrencies very secure. Again, since there is also a limit to the number of transactions that can be carried out in a single day, it might take even days let alone hours to finalize a simple transaction.

Last of all, you always run the risk that the cryptocurrency that you are investing in or trading in is going to bubble and bust and this just comes with any type of natural money but with cryptocurrency, you definitely shouldn't start out by investing everything you own in it because you don't know if the cryptocurrency is going to be worth anything within the next week.

What Bitcoin Fixes

There are a few things that cryptocurrency actually fixes that a lot of banks have problems with and the first of this is the country boundary that has almost always applied to paper money in the past. You see, there are fees included with changing any type of money to any type of money but there are some countries where the change simply isn't possible. For example, companies such as MoneyGram or Western Union charge rates of about 8% to send money from one country to another. Due to the fact that Bitcoin is a universal money, the fees that are applied are simply the fees that are incurred if you go with a service. If you were to trade with someone on a personal level, there's no middle man such as a bank, stocking trade company, or any other type of middleman person that would normally charge you a fee for such an exchange. On a personal level, you can simply hand them Bitcoin and then receive a product without having to pay sales tax or anything like that. Additionally, you have some countries that don't have access to American Banks or things like PayPal and Bitcoin helps overcome this challenge because it bypasses the link, the bureaucratic process of getting a country approved for utilizing another country's type of currency.

Bitcoin is also determined to save people who have to go through dysfunctional banking systems in developing countries. The problem with the conventional banking systems is that they are geographically isolated. This means that if you are an Argentine for instance, you are only expected to use the Argentinean banking system and the same goes to all other countries as well. However, this is the bridge that Bitcoin is looking to gap because its network is global. This benefits mostly the people living in the low income nations who are concerned that their local bank could misappropriate their funds.

One of the most important problem issues that Bitcoin could fix is to improve payment security. The standard credit card network basically employs the honor system and fraud detection only happens after transactions. Bitcoin can therefore be used to operate as the basis for payment systems that deal with fraudulent transactions in a much more sophisticated manner. For instance, if you are trying to push through a transaction through a bitcoin based android payment application, its interface could ask you to approve the transaction before submitting it to the bitcoin network.

The last thing and probably the most important considering the times that we live in is that Bitcoin is a fixed currency, which means that no government can force an inflation or deflation of the Bitcoin currency. As we saw with what happened with the United States government, the inflation of money caused a bubble collapse that resulted in the necessary saving of companies that would have otherwise destabilize the country. This is because the inflation rate didn't match the deflation rate on a much broader spectrum and this was influenced by big companies or at least that's what the conspiracies say. By having a currency that releases new coins every 10 minutes at a set rate for the next century, we can expect and understand the inflation rate that's going to affect us now and within a century.

In the next chapter, we will be discussing how bitcoin has risen over the years since it was founded to become the most valuable cryptocurrency in the world.

Chapter 3: Rise of Bitcoin

Thanks to Coindesk and Coinmarketcap, starting in the year 2013, we can actually see what happened to Bitcoin over that time.

The First Rise

In October of 2013, we saw Bitcoin rise in value dramatically, going from a few tens of dollars to nearly thousands of dollars. Speculators believe that the cause of this rise began earlier in the year with the Banking Crisis in Cyprus where the government forced banks to take the loss that they would incur. In order to avoid this, many smart individuals rushed to their accounts to pull out and push their money into Bitcoin, which is why you saw such a massive spike in Bitcoin. The reason why they did this is because of the anonymity and decentralized nature of Bitcoin, which meant that the government couldn't touch it. This only caused the price of Bitcoin to rise by a couple hundred dollars though before the price dropped again as hackers took to attacking some of the early Bitcoin exchanges. It seems that China caught wind of how important of an investment Bitcoin could be because it was China that brought the prices for Bitcoin up in October and this led to a surge of people trying to get their hands on Bitcoin so they could sell to China. It was during this month that Bitcoin first hit its' thousand dollar marke before climbing back down over time. It would never again go below $100.

The Second Rise

The second rise wouldn't be truly seen until the beginning of 2017, the year in which this book is written. While not as sharp as the first rise, the second rise is still continuing with two bubble-bursts while rising.

Starting in September of 2016, the price of Bitcoin has gone from $600 to nearly $4,800 by October of 2017. Both of the falls resulted in a near 50% loss with the first loss happening in July when the price dropped by nearly $500 and the next happening in September when the price dropped by nearly $1,000 before rising again.

Rising Profits

As more and more people join the network, the rarity of Bitcoin goes up, which means that the price for a BTC goes up. Due to the irregularity of Bitcoin, over time, there is actually a deflation of the cryptocurrency, given that only 21 million Bitcoins can ever be created. This number is less considering that some Bitcoins are lost due to people throwing old computers away when Bitcoin was worthless, loss of key phrases and a lack of care. There have been many stories where individuals disregarded their Bitcoin when it was worthless, only to find out it is worth thousands of dollars today. In some cases, there have been reports that these individuals have gone back to the junk yard to try and recover their old computers, only to find out that their Bitcoins are gone, worth potentially millions of dollars today.

The current Market Cap for Bitcoin is around $80,000,000,000 and this only happened over a decade. You could literally say that Bitcoin exploded into the market.

This explosion could not be possible without bitcoin miners availing the bitcoins to the market.

For a FREE course on how to buy your first Bitcoin, Litecoin, and Ethereum,

Get $10 worth of Bitcoin for free when you register today and invest $100

Chapter 4: Bitcoin Mining

Mining is Various

Bitcoin is created through a process known as Mining. One of the most noticeable parts about Bitcoin mining is that it is as confusing as can be whenever you're first trying to start your mining operation. Even if you are just curious about the technology, it can be confusing because of several different factors. You see, most people think there is only one way to mine Bitcoins because after all, there's really only one way to mine mineral ore and so it would only make sense that there's only one way to mine cryptocurrency but the truth is that there's more than one way. A lot of the confusion has to deal with just what goes into Bitcoin itself. There is more than one way to go about mining Bitcoin and this is where the confusion comes in. You primarily have three different options; solo mining, pool mining, and cloud mining. However, you actually have to understand how you get money from Bitcoin mining itself so let's cover that first before we cover the different ways you can mine.

Bitcoin Mining is a Reward Scheme

The first thing that you need to understand is that Bitcoin mining is actually not mining. It's one of those situations where it sounds like it could be one thing but it's really another thing. Essentially, the Bitcoin Network hands you a key that you need to work on in order to prove that the coin transaction occurred. This key is extremely complicated and the network measures it out so that it will take about 10 minutes to figure out the necessary hash function to validate the existence of those coins. Since Bitcoin transactions are happening all the time, these opportunities to validate coins is escalated to a height that you and I can go about mining these proof of work calculations. The first person who receives a correct version of the proof of work calculation is the person that receives the Bitcoins. There are a few different aspects to these calculations that cause problems with individual users though.

The Calculator Arms Race

You see, the average individual will have a computer that's capable of making billions of calculations every second and that's known as a gigahertz. Once people found that they could make money with this, the competition for the amount of calculations that are possible is significantly higher than it used to be. In the early days when cryptocurrency wasn't that popular, you could just utilize your CPU and generally make some Bitcoins every other day. As it grew in popularity, the calculations to solve the proof of work function became a lot more complicated and so it required a lot more processing power. The obvious first solution is to simply upgrade your hardware or upgrade the way in which you solve the equation. A lot of people spent money on processors because they were able to do the more complex equations at the time that Bitcoin was starting to grow in popularity, but they began to move over to GPUs once GPUs became rather powerful.

Why GPUs

GPU, also known as Graphics Processing Unit, is simply a much faster CPU. You see, with a regular processor, you only have maybe 8 to 32 cores depending on whether you have a mainstream processor or a server processor. Bitcoin miners would buy up as many 32 core server processors as they could possibly fit into a PC and since most server processors would only support up to a maximum of 2 server processors, there wasn't a lot of room for growth. That is until somebody had the bright idea to utilize GPU cores instead of CPU cores. You see, on a GPU you have thousands cores and we're getting to the point where there's going to be millions of simpler processors that handle chunks of calculations. Someone wrote the necessary algorithm to change the hash function so that it can utilize GPU power rather than CPU power. This happened only recently and was the primary cause for many shortages when it came to gamers wanting to buy a GPU to just play games. Since PC Gamers tended to buy the newest on the market and so did Bitcoin miners, the PC Gamers found that they were having a hard time locating top-of-the-line graphics cards because the Bitcoin miners invested a lot more money into purchasing the graphics cards as soon as they were on the market. Therefore, where a GPU Enthusiast that was a PC Gamer would normally buy a single graphics card the Bitcoin miner would buy 100 graphics cards. As you can see, this creates a shortage amongst the graphics cards and it increases the prices of the graphics cards in order to limit the wave of people that need them. However, due to the limitations of how many GPUs were available, we now came out with the technology called ASIC.

The New ASIC

ASIC stands for Application Specific Integrated Circuit and a lot of people are still really puzzled as to why this is better than a GPU. I'm going to come out and say that this is a battle between Generalized versus Specified. That may still be confusing, so let's use some search algorithms to see an example of where specification really matters. In computer science, we have Linear search and Binary search. Let's say we have a group of numbers from one to a hundred. If you don't know where twenty-five is, you would likely count from one to twenty-five. It is a slow and arduous task, but it will eventually get the job done. This is called Linear search and it is only useful when you have no idea where the numbers are organized such as : 1, 9, 89, 2. This is how a single GPU core is designed because it doesn't really know what is going to go where until it is done with a calculation. As you can imagine, such a Linear search is unreasonable when dealing with one person (a GPU core) and numbers that reach into the trillions. If you know the exact pattern of the numbers though, such as being ordered from one to a hundred, you can then run a Binary search instead. This is similar to how we see a Hash Function or Proof of Work function and an ASIC. A Binary search means that you continuously divide your search group in half and then see if it is more than one group and less than one group, going with the group that is less than. Therefore, on the search to twenty-five, you would divide the group in half, which would give you fifty, and see if twenty-five is more or less than fifty. Since it is less than fifty, we would throw out the more group and use the less group. Since twenty-five is the middle of the less group, we're done and it only took 2 steps instead of 25. ASIC is specifically built to only solve the Proof of Work function, which makes it extremely efficient there and useless everywhere else. A GPU is generalized so it can do the Proof of Work function *alright* but it can also do everything else *alright*.

Electricity

Now if you're wondering where the profit is made, you should be looking at the amount of electricity that it costs to actually run the hardware and software that will mine the Bitcoin for you. You see a lot of people like to jump into this big old pile of Bitcoin mining because they see the price tag on how much a Bitcoin is worth, but the truth is that mining it can actually be more expensive than the actual Bitcoin. Let's walk through an example. Let's say that a Bitcoin is worth $1,000. Let's say that it takes you about a year to get a full Bitcoin from all the mining that you do because you are likely to join a pool rather than solo mine. Let's say that it takes about 1 kilowatt an hour to run your mining operation at around $0.10 an hour. By running your system for a full 24 hours a day 365 days out of the year, you will have spent $864 on just the electricity. In other words, if you manage to make a Bitcoin that you can sell for $1,000, you will only have made about $140 in profit. This is what it means to judge whether your system is profitable enough for you to make any money off of it. Not only that, but the amount of money that it costs to actually buy the system necessary for the Bitcoin isn't even $140. Normally, such a system that would grant you a high enough reward that you could claim at least $1,000 a year is in the thousand dollars and higher range. This is why you need to make sure that it is actually profitable for you to mine before you go about doing it because you could easily dig yourself a hole without realizing it. The reason why some countries are building mining farms is because they have either built a system that runs entirely off of solar or the electricity costs so little that it only takes a very small portion out of their profit range.

One of the biggest players in Bitcoin Mining is Genesis Mining. Genesis mining works based on contracts. You can purchase different mining contracts, for example, Bitcoin contracts, which are an open ended contract. This means that the contract lasts forever as long as Bitcoin is profitable to mine. It is currently the most popular and profitable contract to date. Genesis mining promises a daily payout in any cryptocurrency of your choice. This form of mining is more profitable as there is no overhead costs such as electricity and maintenance.

For more information check out. https://www.genesis-mining.com/

For a 3% discount, use this code on ANY contracts: apS1YL

Pools

The primary way that people make money off of Bitcoin is by farming inside of pools. A pool refers to a collection of computers on a network that are all trying to solve the problem. The reason why this is the primary way is because everyone devotes their Bitcoin machines to solving a block code, the reward, and the first person who solves it splits the Bitcoin money amount amongst all the people inside of the pool. This means that it doesn't matter how powerful your system is; if your system is the one responsible for solving the code first then you hand out the Bitcoin reward in equal portions to everybody else. With that said, a lot of people don't see the benefit until they realize that finding the block code is different than solving the block. Someone else in your network might actually find the block code before you do but because your machine is more powerful than theirs, you are able to solve it. This is the primary benefit that comes with working in pools and there are several different pools to work in.

Worker

The term worker is used whenever people are talking about their processors and you set up a worker to run at a specific frequency so then you can actually get some calculations done. Essentially, whenever you hear the term worker, people are most likely talking about their entire system if they haven't set up several workers to take advantage of several different pools. Usually, the average individual will only have a single worker that's running on a single piece of hardware. However, if you build something like a Raspberry Pi Farm to handle multiple different processors then you are likely going to have as many workers as you do Raspberry Pi's.

How to Mine Bitcoin

Now there are several different ways you can actually mine your Bitcoins and there are benefits and downsides to each of them. The important thing to realize here is that almost all of them implement themselves in the same way. This is where I'm going to tell you how you actually mine your Bitcoins. First of all, you get a Bitcoin account and the most common place to start out is actually bitcoinmining.com or slushpool.com. If you do not want to mine Bitcoins yourself, you will need to go to a Bitcoin mining pool website like slushpool.com. The software that is commonly used for mining is BFGMiner, CGMiner, and libblkmaker. Many of these will lead you down a path of code found on Github, but navigating around a bit will lead you to version software. For simplicity sake, we're going to go down the path of Slush Pool.

1. You will need to setup an account with them like you would with any website really. You will have a user name and a worker name. For instance, TMkeg.worker1.

2. For Slush Pool, you will need either cgminer or BFGminer. With both of them, the directions are pretty much the same. Bfgminer.org will come out directly to a download page where you can download either Windows 32bit or Windows 64bit, or one of five supported linux distros. CGminer requires you to go to the Readme where you will find a section called "Downloads" and following the link will lead you to a bunch of

different versions of CGminer. Once you download either zip, you will extract it, find their executables, and run them.

3. Running the executable, you will be asked to enter 3 different items: URL, userID, and password. The userID is a combination of your Slush Pool username and worker name. The password is the password to the account. The URL, on the other hand, is found here: https://slushpool.com/help/get-started/getting started. The url is regional so there are five possible URLs you could enter, but it is up to you to choose the best one.

4. Once you enter that in, your CMD software is connected to the network and, provided you have an ASIC device, it will begin mining.

As you can see, this is relatively easy to implement once you get past all the jargon but the problem is that this is only one way of doing it. This is called pool mining and pools have requirements. You cannot join Slush Pool without having an ASIC device due to the high demands of today's Bitcoin market. I mean, we're talking about Peta hashes nowadays. To give you a clue about how huge this is, 1,000 Terabytes is a Petabyte.

Solo Mining

Solo mining is a little bit different but instead of pointing it at a pool, you point it at yourself. You see, all the pool is doing is pointing all the processing power into a single location so while somebody in Wyoming might have a farm of machines working on this, your computer will be pointed in the same direction as that person in Wyoming. All it is doing is pointing your machines towards a single network access point. Therefore, in order to mine the Bitcoins yourself you just need to point it towards your device and so you're using the same miner software but you're setting it up with your own username, your own password, and your own pool. The username and password can be anything that you want but the pool is something different. The pool is your IP address and the port number that you set your GPU up on so that it doesn't confuse it with the GPU that your computer is using. In order to make this change so that your miner opens up to mining on your GPU automatically, you have to make a configuration file. For example, if I go into my cgminer-4.0.0 folder, I will find an example.conf file that I can open up with a Text Editor (not Word, but something like Notepad++) and see how my configuration file should be written. In order to find out what you need inside of it, you should definitely look at the code repository for your version of your miner. This is the hardest form of mining and the one with the least amount of payoff for anyone who doesn't have a football-sized Bitcoin farm.

Pool Mining

I've already explained how pool mining really works on a core level but here I'm going to actually elaborate on what I mean. You see, the people that you are pooling your resources with and the reason why it is called a pool is that it is handling all the network connections to solve bits of code. Imagine, if you will, a server farm that has a whole bunch of network connections interconnecting the servers but ultimately serves a singular purpose. This is what a pool does for the Bitcoin Network. This community has a singular network access point to the Bitcoin Network and you are part of a group of people (known as a pool) that is sharing that singular network access point. By doing this, the work that the Bitcoin Network requires of your machine is spread out amongst everyone who is a part of the pool. This is why when anyone manages to break the code inside of the pool, everyone inside of the pool gets a piece of the Bitcoin.

Bitcoin Mining Clouds

Now that you know what pool mining is, you might wonder what cloud mining is and how it is different from pool mining. It pretty much serves the same purpose but not everyone has access to the devices that are specific to certain types of pools. The ASIC requirement set forth by Splash Pool can't really be met by everyone who's trying to get into the industry just for the kicks of it. Anyone that's wanting a thousandth of a Bitcoin and can only afford their own computer will not want to buy a $600 - $1,000 machine. This is how Cloud mining was brought about because people who cannot pay for the device can rent one via the cloud so that they can just start up their own mining without having to do much. This ensures quality control, speed, and rate that also allows the company holding the cloud mining business model to expand and get more power. The problem is that some people will fall for traps when it comes to others who make it seem like they have a cloud mining operation but are just fooling people into believing that they have one while also collecting all the money that people invest into their business. After all, someone isn't going to notice that they don't actually have any Bitcoins until they submit a withdrawal request and then the person who owns the website can easily shut down the account without a reason and just evaporate into space.

Other Ways To Acquire Bitcoins

You already know that new bitcoins are created through the process of mining. But over the years, the bitcoin network has really grown and thus mining is now proving to become a very technologically complex task than it was since its inception. For most new users, it is virtually impractical to mine new bitcoins.

That is why there is the easier and better alternative to acquire bitcoins and that is by purchasing it from other people who already have them.

Buying bitcoins with your cash also has its own advantages. For example, it is not only easier than mining but it is also done privately and swiftly. This is because most exchanges will not demand that you to reveal your identity or give out critical information about yourself. Additionally, converting your money to bitcoin only takes a few hours and you are good to go.

There are a few ways to purchase such bitcoins. First of all, there are what we call Bitcoin exchanges. A bitcoin exchange is a digital marketplace that allows traders to sell or buy bitcoins using a variety of currencies. It is therefore an online platform that functions as an intermediary between the sellers and the buyers of any form of cryptocurrency.

One of the most popular exchanges includes Coinbase, which trades bitcoins for euros and US dollars. The trade is made all the more easier because the company has developed mobile smart phone apps to facilitate the exchanges. Another exchange is the Unocoin, which focuses solely on the Indian market. To trade using this exchange, you must register yourself with a PAN (Permanent Account Number) card. Last but not least is Circle. This exchange allows traders all around the globe to send, acquire and also store bitcoins. Basically, the best exchange option depends on the country or region you come from. Basically there are many exchanges globally. This is a list of some of them and the mode of payment options that are allowed for each.

There are also websites that allow bitcoin traders who are interested in making bitcoin exchanges in person to find one another in their local areas. One of the websites that makes this possible is localbitcoins.com.

Lastly, most people can now buy and sell their cash for bitcoins using Bitcoin ATMs. It was not until the year 2013 that this new exchange mode was introduced. Basically, these ATMs were introduced to make it even easier and faster to sell or buy Bitcoins while also marketing further the idea of Bitcoin and therefore making it more accessible to many people.

It is recommended that you use the exchanges in the above list or conduct a thorough research before engaging in a trade through any exchange. This is because it has come to our attention that a growing number of sham exchanges are run by fraudsters whose aim is to acquire your personal information or details such as your digital key.

As you dip your feet into bitcoin mining or purchasing bitcoins, you will need a way of keeping/storing your bitcoins i.e. you will need a wallet. Let's discuss bitcoin wallets next.

Bitcoin Wallets

A bitcoin wallet is essentially what you might describe as a bank account for your bitcoins. This is because a wallet allows you to send, acquire and store bitcoins. Without a wallet, you cannot do any of these things. Therefore, a bitcoin wallet is the 1st step for you to start using bitcoins.

The function of wallets is to hold your secret codes (private keys) that allow you to spend bitcoins. In actual sense, it is not the bitcoins that you need to store and safeguard but rather your personal keys that allow you access to the bitcoins.

With this in mind, a wallet can either be a physical device (hardware), an application (software) or a website.

Hardware Wallets

It is any tangible/physical electronic gadget that is designed for the sole function of storing and safeguarding bitcoins. What makes hardware wallets to be secure than other wallet types is that you must connect the device to a computer, tablet or smartphone to spend them. Their purpose is to keep your private keys away from the susceptible internet connected devices. With hardware wallets, you can be sure that your private keys are well kept in a protected offline environment that is very secure even if the hardware were to be connected to a computer infected with malware.

This mode of generating and keeping private keys away from the internet makes sure that cyber criminals have absolutely no chance of sniffing their noses anywhere near your bitcoins. The only option for them is to physically steal the hardware itself, but still it will be useless for them because it is usually protected with a PIN security code that is only known to you.

The three most popular hardware wallets include Trezor, KeepKey and the Ledger Nano S. When you go shopping for a hardware wallet, it is advisable that you purchase one with a screen on it. This is because the screen offers extra security by not only displaying but also verifying crucial wallet details. Basically, this screen is more trustworthy than the information displayed on your computer monitor. One of the most popular hardware wallet is the Ledger Nano S. For more information, visit wonpublications.com/ledger

Hot Wallets

Hot wallets are the opposite of what we may refer to as 'cold storage' of bitcoins. You could compare cold storage of bitcoins to how banks move their client funds into a safe or vault instead of keeping them at the bank tellers' booth. In simple terms, a hot wallet is basically a software that you install on your internet connected device such as a tablet, phone or computer. Hot wallets are different to cold storage in that they are constantly connected to the internet. Hot wallets ensure that every bitcoin transaction keeps some sort of liquidity just in the event that there happens to be massive flood of withdrawal requests. Liquidity in this case can be likened to the cash reserves that any bank should have to make it convenient for the clients to access their funds at any time and point. This type of Bitcoin storage also ensures that you are in complete control of the security of your bitcoins. The only problem is that you store these coins on your computer that is connected to the internet and that leaves them more susceptible to cyber theft.

You could liken a hot wallet to your physical cash wallet that you carry around in your pockets because you can access it easily from there. You only use your cash wallet to keep some little cash but not all your life savings. In this case, hot wallets are used for temporarily storing small amounts of bitcoins where they can be withdrawn instantly if the need arises. They are also convenient if you like to make frequent payments. This means that receiving payments and spending your bitcoins using hot wallets is not only fast but it's also very easy.

As stated earlier, when using the hot wallet, you face the big risk of unrecoverable theft if it so happens that your device is hacked. Due to this vulnerability, you are advised to never keep huge amounts of bitcoin in your hot wallet. The hardware wallets are much more suited for that kind of task. Actually, many of the bitcoin losses suffered as a result of hacking can be attributed to the poor security practices of storing bitcoins in hot wallets.

Many trustworthy service providers that offer bitcoin withdrawal of any sort are known for keeping an extremely little number of bitcoins in their hot wallets. This enables them to carry out instant withdrawals of limited typical quantities. This means that they usually forced into a delay coupled with some manual job to carry out a bigger withdrawal because the funds have to be fetched from alternative storages.

One of the most common wallets for desktop computers is Electrum. This is a light weight software wallet that you can download and install on your computer. Released in the year 2011, Electrum is compatible with Windows, Linux and Mac operating systems. What makes it so popular is that it supports the various hardware wallets such as KeepKey and Trezor.

In case your computer hard drive gets stolen or corrupted, or worse still the whole computer is hacked, then the safety of your bitcoins is left hanging in the balance. This is the reason why you have to be well prepared for such happenings by installing a backup software. Moreover, it would also be wise if you try implementing some safety procedures such as a wallet address rotation. In a nutshell, it would be more safer to use such a wallet if you are tech-savvy.

You can also get wallets for smartphones such as Airbitz, breadwallet, mycelium and GreenBits.

Web/Online Wallets

These are basically web hosted wallets that you can access through your web browser just like you would with any other website. These websites store your private keys and you can access them from any place on planet earth provided that there is internet connectivity. Again, it is not advisable to keep a large number of bitcoins in your web wallet because the risk of cyber theft is high in such a platform. The best thing to do is to store them in cold storage.

Using the web based wallets to store your bitcoins means that you are entrusting third party companies to safeguard them for you. Therefore, you have to be wise enough to choose a reliable and trustworthy provider to store your bitcoins. Examples include: green address, BitGo and Blockchain.info.

The advantage with this kind of wallets is that the service providers take care of your overall wallet security for you including backing them up and implementing address rotations for you. You see, there is no online company that would like to have its reputation tarnished and risk losing clients because it is prone to cyber attacks. They will go an extra mile if need be to cement their status as the best in the business. It is up to you to choose whoever you think will be a reliable bitcoin wallet provider. And how exactly will you identify a secure bitcoin wallet? If they satisfy the following qualities, then they are trustworthy and reliable:

First of all, a reliable service provider puts great emphasis on security over anything else. And there are three ways they do this:

- If they are compliant with the DPA (data protection acts). Make sure that you contact your local data protection legislators and gauge the degree of compliance that that particular company offers.

- If they are able to conduct a device authorization test. They should be able to monitor your browser as well as the device you use so as to lock out any unauthorized access to your funds.

- If they a have a 2 factor verification before clearance. A trustworthy company will ask you for more authorization through an SMS to verify that it is really you logging in.

- And finally, if they encourage you to use strong passwords. If the service provider is as reliable as they say, they will usually warn you to always set strong passwords. For instance, using a 12 bit encryption password. Though some of the companies may be somehow lenient about such a security measure, that might not be perceived as a flaw on their part but it certainly takes off a few points to their security scoreboard.

Apart from security, you should also find an online wallet that offers an array of services for convenience. And one of the most important is probably the debit card as it makes sure that you develop further the manner in which you spend your money. For example, you may need to shop online and request for a delivery for a certain product. Due to the fact that finding a delivery service that accepts bitcoins is rare, you could solve that problem by using a plastic card. That's the beauty of debit cards. They can also enable you to verify accounts and also help you shop online without the need for ever going through a merchant who accepts bitcoins.

A reliable service provider is very transparent about the various costs they charge for withdrawals, transfers and processing deposits. Trustworthy companies go further with their transparency by making clear and open the details about the technicalities of new features. If there is any company that offers anything to the contrary, then you should just write them off as dodgy schemes.

Online wallets should be able to process speedy Bitcoin payments or payments using other currencies make sure you identify the number of countries where the wallet is fully functional and also take note of the limitations as well. As you research, look for the average time it takes to process payments. Arguably, the best way to research on this issue is to search for testimonials on independent media platforms such as Reddit.

And finally, make sure that you claim the full control over your bitcoins before you entrust your funds to a stranger online. When looking for a trustworthy wallet, ensure that they guarantee you the freedom to use it. This means that you should look for an online wallet that gives you secure and free withdrawals and money deposits wherever and whenever you need to. A reliable web wallet has nothing to fear or hide and they should be able to provide a continuous day or night access to the complete operational control of your funds. However, many companies will limit your withdrawal or deposits to only a few satoshi; the least amount being 0.0001 satoshi.

Paper Wallets

This is basically a printed piece of paper that holds information including the private key and a cryptocurrency address both of which are encrypted in the form of a QR code and can be decoded by a QR reader. Instead of saving those long series of characters on your computer drive that make up the private key, some people deem it fit to print the key instead and keep the paper in a safe place. Paper wallets are preferred to software or online wallets because like the hardware wallets, they are considered to be more secure for storing huge quantities of Bitcoin.

The advantage of using a paper wallet is that it is more or less like using a cold storage because it can't be connected to the internet and as a result, it cannot be hacked. Also unlike hardware wallets, they are a way cheaper alternative for cold storage.

Generating a non secure paper wallet is a rather simple task. Just visit the BitAddress website and generate your private key. Next click on the 'paper wallet' link and then print it. This is the wrong way to generate your paper wallet and DO NOT attempt to use follow it because it is non-secure.

The problem with this method is that you are connected to the internet as you carry out the process. And this means that people might be able to monitor whatever is happening on your screen. And this is true especially if you are using a computer running on Windows operating system because it is more susceptible to malware. Furthermore, if someone manages to hack the BitAddress website, he/she will have the chance to pick up all the private keys that people generate.

So what is the correct method? If you're truly determined to protect your bitcoins by generating a secure paper wallet, this is the due process to be followed. It may be a bit complex and tiresome but ultimately, it is worth every effort:

Make sure you download the essential tools and these include the BitAddress app, the Linux live app and the Ubuntu o/s.

Now install Ubuntu on your flash disk. This will delete everything else that is on the disk. Next launch the Linux Live and plug in the flash disk. Select the drive on your computer. if the icon does not appear, click refresh or hit F5 on the keyboard. Open the 'ISO/IMG/ZIP' folder and then click on the Ubuntu ISO file you downloaded in step 1. At this juncture, ensure that only the 'format the key oin FAT32' is highlighted. When all that is done, click on the lightning bolt icon to begin installation.

When installation is complete, now unzip the BitAddress and also copy it into the flash disk. The next and most crucial step is to **disconnect** the computer from the internet. Ensure that there isn't any remote access to your device. To run your PC using Ubuntu from the flash disk, hit F1 or F12 on your keyboard. A new page will appear. On it, click on the 'try Ubuntu option.

Now you have to make sure that your printer is synchronized with the new Ubuntu o/s so that you may be able to print. To do this, click on the 'cog wheel' and 'monkey wrench' icon to launch the system settings window. Select 'printers' then 'add'. Now you can synchronize your printer with the operating system. To check if it's working, print a test page.

The final step is to launch the BitAddress you downloaded and generate your own paper wallet on your PC's hard drive. To do this launch Mozilla Firefox, then right click and select 'open a new private window'. When the window appears, click on the address bar and type in:

File:///cdrom/bitaddress.org-master/

And press enter. On the next window, click Bitaddress.org.html.

To generate the wallet, move the cursor until the reading on the top right comes to 0. Now select 'paper wallet' from the menu and then print it. Congratulations, you have now created your paper wallet.

This process is considered to be a more secure because:

- You use the offline version of BitAddress meaning that it can't be hacked.

- You're using an Ubuntu operating system which is an 'out-of-the-box' strategy that is better equipped to fend off malware than Windows.

- And finally, you are disconnected to the internet while your private key is being processed.

Now that you know how to mine bitcoins and keep them secure in a wallet, the next part we will discuss is how to use bitcoins.

Chapter 5: How Bitcoin Is Used As Money

One of the first things that people think about whenever they think about Bitcoin is how it can be used as a currency rather than a stock item. While a great portion of the market is dedicated to the trading of Bitcoins with real currency, there is an equally large amount of individuals who utilized Bitcoins as actual currency so as to buy things such as a car or a coffee shop. There are a number of individuals who have purchased Lamborghinis and mansions solely by using Bitcoins.

Direct Transfer

One of the most obvious ways that Bitcoin is utilized as money is by directly transferring it to other Bitcoin users. Primarily, when a Bitcoin user wants to transfer over Bitcoins to another user they have to get their public key and utilize their digital wallets to transfer the Bitcoins over to that individual. You can store the Bitcoins on your computer and physically send them yourself but the process is rather complicated. Direct transfers are usually used simply because of how much easier it makes everything whenever you're trying to buy something such as a community couch or a car but the most common reason why someone would transfer Bitcoins is actually to purchase a service, but some services are not sold via Bitcoin and so some individuals will trade Bitcoins on a personal level so that they can bypass an online purchase scheme. An example of this would be a wallet that first converts the Bitcoins into the necessary currency that's going to be utilized by the service before transferring over the money so that even though the user has Bitcoins, the seller receives the currency that they are looking for.

Market Exchange

As we've already mentioned, some individuals decide to gamble inside of other cryptocurrencies besides Bitcoin and it's important to realize that you can exchange cryptocurrencies for other cryptocurrencies. If you think that a certain cryptocurrency is likely to be better than another, you can exchange your current cryptocurrency for that cryptocurrency that you're looking for. This doesn't happen a lot with the mainstream cryptocurrency as of right now but that isn't to say that it doesn't happen and that isn't to say that it won't happen in the future when other cryptocurrencies that are more trusted than Bitcoin come along to take over the market. Additionally, some users only trust a certain kind of cryptocurrency in an area so even though Bitcoin is trusted in most areas of the world, that doesn't mean that there aren't areas that refuse to accept Bitcoin and will only take certain cryptocurrencies that they produced themselves. As I said, this isn't really a common aspect to cryptocurrency market exchange but the honest truth is that it does happen.

However, a more likely scenario of a market exchange is if someone has had Bitcoins for a long period of time where they bought them at a significantly cheaper amount of money and now they're trying to pay out in order to get more currency such as the United States dollar or the Japanese Yen. This is the more common type of market exchange and it happens all the time when people buy low and then sell high, which is a tactic used by traders all over the world in the regular stock market. However, that doesn't mean that you're going to get the amount of money that you want all the time but the most common practice that people have is that they will buy Bitcoin when it's a very low price and wait until it's a very high price or until they see that they can make pennies on the dollar.

Services

As I've already mentioned, some individuals actually utilize Bitcoin as paying for a service like you would find on Amazon or Ebay. Due to the fact that there are no boundaries for Bitcoin, it becomes very handy when you live in a country that places large fees on money going in or money coming out or both ways. This means that individuals who are looking to avoid the nasty fees that normally come with exchanging foreign currency will likely go after the Bitcoin advantage of being a Global Currency. For this very reason, a lot of black market trades usually occur utilizing Bitcoin simply because it can go into a person's wallet without leaving a digital footprint behind it beyond the username of who owns the Bitcoin. That means that Bitcoins can be exchanged by literally handing over somebody's hard drive rather than holding onto millions of dollars inside of a briefcase. That isn't to say that unscrupulous people will use the anonymous aspect of Bitcoin but that is how it has become so infamous. Meanwhile, perfectly respectable people utilize this aspect on a daily basis simply because it is much easier to run exchanges by having a currency that isn't limited to borders.

Discounted Service

Another aspect that a lot of people have come to appreciate is that the value of Bitcoin increases over time with a rather High chance of success. Due to the fact that a lot of people realize that the value of Bitcoin increases over time, in order to get more customers that they can get a higher profit in the long run certain companies will actually provide you a discount if you utilize Bitcoins instead of real world currency so that they can gain more Bitcoins that will increase in value over time. This is a very small Niche part of the market but it does happen and a lot of people at take advantage of this. It is one of the best ways to utilize Bitcoin as a currency I rather than a stock option.

With all that in mind, the next chapter will focus on the benefits and risks that come with investing in bitcoins.

Chapter 6: Benefits And Risks Of Bitcoin Investing

Peer Value

The first attribute of Bitcoin that is both a risk and a benefit is that the value of Bitcoin is set by your peers. The risk is that your peers will no longer see any value inside of Bitcoin and so Bitcoin will lose any type of material worth, which means that if you invested thousands of dollars inside of Bitcoin then you would lose thousands of dollars as a result. However, that is also the benefit of Bitcoin. Since your peers can determine the level of value that's inside of a Bitcoin, this allows the market value of Bitcoin to become obscenely high at certain periods of time and then drop extremely low when everybody has been buying up for a while. This is how people generally make money and it's very close to gambling. This also increases the overall worth of Bitcoin due to the fact that the more people who are invested in Bitcoin means that there are more Bitcoins that are spread around and the value of Bitcoin goes up as a result. A good example of this is that Bitcoin used to only cost a total of $0 and now you can expect to spend over $14,000 to just get one Bitcoin. This is because the popularity of Bitcoin has gone up and this means that the overall value of Bitcoin has gone up as a result of this. Therefore, it's kind of like it could go wrong at any moment but you're hoping that it doesn't.

Sell Short

One of the benefits about Bitcoin is that you can sell short pretty quickly and this doesn't mean a lot unless you're used to trading in the regular stock markets. Selling short means that you can buy stocks or items when they are low and after waiting a short period of time, you can then turn around and sell those items to make a profit by raising those prices by a few cents or a few dollars. A lot of people don't think that trading like this can actually make you a lot of money but let's say that you have 100 Bitcoins and you bought them at $50 even, each. Now let's say that you waited for a couple of days and now those Bitcoins have become worth $60. That means if you decide to sell them at $10 extra a piece, you effectively made $1,000 in just a couple of days.

Sell Long

Just like you have selling short you also have selling long, which refers to the option of buying stocks when they are low price and selling them much later on in the life of the stock once the stock has reached a high enough price. A good example of this is buying stocks when they were maybe $5 to $20 a piece and trying to get as much of the stock as you possibly can. You wait a couple of years after you've bought this stock and suddenly you see that Bitcoin has made a bubble where you are watching the prices climb into the thousands of dollars. You can then automatically go straight into selling each of the stuff that you bought and easily make close to 15 to 22 and even $500,000 simply because you bought them at a low price when they first came out and waited until they became of suddenly high. This occurs whenever there's a bubble and we'll talk about this in a little bit.

Trust Issues

As I already mentioned, Bitcoin heavily relies on the trust that goes into it and since the professionals of the cryptology industry have certified that it would be incredibly difficult to hack Bitcoin, the value of Bitcoin goes up. The problem is that if anyone manages to hack

Bitcoin and gains the system then it all falls apart because the value of Bitcoin is reliant on how trustworthy Bitcoin network can be and if Bitcoin can't be trusted, then there is no more value inside of Bitcoin. Essentially, if somebody were to break the Bitcoin system then all of your Bitcoins would become almost useless overnight.

New Value Every Ten Minutes

People think that Bitcoin would become a stagnant market if it didn't constantly produce new Bitcoins or would become a novelty item that only the rich could afford but luckily for us, Bitcoin releases new coins every 10 minutes and it will do this for the next century. This means that the market will continuously get more coins that can be mined, found and utilized in the online space, which means that Bitcoin is likely to not be shortened by a lack of Bitcoins. The problem with this, even though it is a fantastic benefit, is that this means Bitcoin will not have an average value for a very long time. There are only so many dollar bills and we stop printing them unless we actually have to print and there are only so many European bills and they stop printing those if they have to, but Bitcoin is automatically set to release new Bitcoins without any interference whatsoever. This means that if Bitcoins become inflated, it is only by the market that they become deflated and this causes a huge problem in the economic view because since you can't control the deflation of a Bitcoin like you can a dollar, the crashes that come from a massive inflation of Bitcoin are much harsher than the crashes you might see in the United States dollar. For example, there have been two times recently within the past few years where the price of Bitcoin was cut in half. If the US dollar experienced something like this within two years, the US would be devastated and thrown back into a third world country.

Market Bubbles

This brings us to our last aspect when it comes to the risks and benefits of Bitcoin currency, which is to say that Bitcoin is very easy when it comes to market bubbles. A market bubble is whenever the inflation rate has risen so much that experts expect the bubble to pop and Bitcoin has quite obviously shown that it will pop. Bitcoin was worth tens of dollars a couple of years ago and now it's up to over 14,000 dollars. Originally, it began as being free and yet people are paying hundreds of dollars for a whole bunch of ones and zeros. The Bitcoin Market is a bit crazy but also understandable because it's almost the same as the markets for the US dollar and for the European dollar, but the Bitcoin isn't controlled by any singular government and runs on its own. This is why a lot of people are in this industry and like to trade Bitcoins back and forth. As you can tell, almost all the benefits that come with Bitcoin also have risks that come with Bitcoin. You'll see that is a very common trend when it comes to bitcoin currency exchanging.

If you would like to know more about cryptocurrency investing, check out my previous book, *'Cryptocurrency: 5 Expert Secrets For Beginners: Investing Into Bitcoin, Ethereum And Litecoin'*. In this book, I cover all the basics of cryptocurrencies and essential information experts use when investing into cryptocurrencies. Learn these tips today.
https://www.amazon.com/dp/B07571MSY5

Although I touched on the next topic earlier, I believe it is important to discuss it in detail so you know just how you can get bitcoins to get started if you haven't.

Chapter 7: Ways To Get Bitcoin

Buying Bitcoin with Fiat Money

The most obvious of all of these is to simply spend cash that you've earned doing whatever that you do on Bitcoins rather than mining for them or trying to sell a product for them. Once you buy Bitcoins, you can then do Bitcoin trading where you will either sell short or sell long and becomes almost identical to stock trading. A common website where you can do this is Coinbase where you can buy the Bitcoins outright with money and then begin trading around. Coinbase is a simple exchange I would highly recommend for first time investors.

Selling Product for Bitcoin

Whether you're an online retailer or a coffee shop in Bangladesh, you can sell your products for Bitcoin. This is a primary way that individuals accumulate Bitcoins because many people simply seek out Bitcoins due to their worth and value. By staying on top of the market and having the ability to sell for Bitcoins, you not only get paid for the products that you're selling but the money that you receive actually grows in value rather than decreases in value, which is a common trend with some of the Fiat money that is around today. In addition to this, you can go out and sell on Craigslist or some other website that allows you to control what type of money you are requesting. This means that you can sell a car, a house, or anything that you could think up of for Bitcoins rather than paper money. This is a very common way to gather Bitcoins since a lot of people don't want to dive into Bitcoin mining and the amount of work it takes to actually retrieve Bitcoins from the system.

Work for Bitcoins

Don't forget that Bitcoin represents money and since money often represents labor, this means you can trade Bitcoins for labor and labor for Bitcoins. There are websites like Coinality that will allow you to trade your work for Bitcoins rather than United States dollars or any type of currency that you're used to working for. Due to the fact that Bitcoin is around $14,800 as of writing this book, you won't get a lot of Bitcoins by accepting some of these jobs and almost all of these jobs are freelance rather than full-time simply because of the nature of Bitcoins.

Debit or Credit cards

Buying bitcoins with credit or debit cards is one of the most common way to pay online. This is largely due to the fact that credit cards are a mode of payment that most people are familiar with and also it is of the easiest methods of buying bitcoins on the internet. The advantage of using this mode of payment is that you will receive your bitcoins immediately the verification process is complete. You can buy bitcoins anywhere in the world using your credit or debit card using Coinmama or CEX.IO. In European countries, you can but through BitPanda. Coinbase enables you to buy bitcoins with your credit/debit card in the whole of Europe, the USA, Singapore and Canada.

Coinbase in particular is the largest bitcoin broker in the world. You can buy up to €150 or $150 worth of bitcoins per week. Additionally, they charge a flat rate of 3.99% on all bitcoins you purchase using a debit or credit card. This fee is one of the cheapest for customers living in the United States and the European continent. Coinbase is offering free bitcoin worth €10 or $10 if you purchase bitcoin exceeding €100. You should know that coinbase only accepts Mastercard and Visa debit/credit cards as of now.

The process of buying bitcoins through Coinbase is simple. First you need to create and account and also add your personal details for login purposes. The site will ask you to upload a copy of your ID. Once that is done, click on your name situated on the top right corner of the window that appears. Now click on the 'settings' tab on the top of the window to launch a drop down menu. On that menu, click on "payment methods" then "add payment method" then credit/ debit card. On the window that appears, key in your credit/debit card details then hit 'enter'. You will receive a confirmation message that tells you that you have succesfully added a card. Now you are ready to buy your bitcoins. Hit enter again. There is a widget on the window that appears afterwards. Simply key in the amount of bitcoins you wish to buy then click "buy bitcoin instantly". Immediately after clicking, your bitcoins will be delivered to your preferred wallet.

Buying Through Bank Transfer Or Bank Account

In most countries, this is one of the best ways to purchase bitcoin. And these are some of the reasons. First of all, paying through bank transfers does not require a lot of fees and it is therefore cost friendly if you compare with other modes of payment. Another advantage is that this method allows you to buy huge amounts of bitcoins.

There are a few downsides however if this is your preferred mode of payment. It is usually a slow process because for instance in North America, a single bank transfer may usually take a maximum of 5 days before you receive your bitcoins. Again, it requires you to verify using your ID and therefore not a good choice if you are concerned about your privacy. You can buy bitcoins via your bank account using BitPanda in the USA, Gemini in the whole of North America and Coinbase in the USA, Europe, Singapore and Canada.

Buying bitcoins with PayPal

Purchasing bitcoins using PayPal is a complex and confusing process. But you shouldn't worry as I'll walk you through the entire process. The first thing you need to know is that PayPal utilizes the services of VirWox to buy bitcoins. It is impossible to buy bitcoins directly using PayPal. But VirWox is not technically a sort of Bitcoin exchange. This is because it is the equivalent of a market for second life lindens which is basically a form of currency used in the virtual world. The idea therefore is to buy SLLs (Second Life Lindens) from VirWox and then sell exchange them for bitcoins.

To buy bitcoins, you first need to open an account on VirWox by visiting the website. Once the page has been launched, key in your details to create an account. Most people get confused by a certain part named 'link to avatar' its not important though and you can leave it for now. Launch your email once you're registered to retrieve a temporary password that you will use to login to your VirWox account. On the window that opens, click on 'change settings' tab located on the left sidebar. This will allow you to change the password to your preferred password but ensure it is strong because it is your money you're dealing with. If you fail to change the password within a day, the accounted will be deleted. Once you've changed the password, click on 'deposit' located on the left sidebar. Scroll down until you find the option that allows you to key in the amount of money you need to deposit. Click on 'checkout with PayPal' button. Login to your PayPal and verify your balance. Now you'll need to exchange the money for

SLLs. To do this, key on the amount of money you want to exchange and hit 'enter'. On the top left, you will see your balance in SLL. Click on 'BTC/SLL' to enable the exchange to take place. Now key in the amount of BTC you want to buy and click 'next'. Now you should be able to see your bitcoins balance on the top left of your monitor.

Gambling

It's almost comical to know that whenever there's any type of money involved, you can almost guarantee that gambling has been on the path sometime during its creation. I don't think that there is a single money system on this planet that doesn't have gambling as a part of it. This is true of Bitcoin because you go on websites and gamble your actual money and they will pay you out in Bitcoins rather than currency. Due to the fact that there are no border limits to Bitcoins, it makes it much easier for gambling websites to give you Bitcoins rather than the currency denomination of your country.

Mining Altcoin for Bitcoin

Ironic as it may sound, it is actually easier in some cases to mine for alternative cryptocurrencies versus mining directly for Bitcoin itself. This is because there are a lower amount of individuals investing their time in the alternative cryptocurrencies and so those cryptocurrency values are still on the rise while Bitcoin is abnormally high. This means that you can race towards those Bitcoins with relative ease by using alternative cryptocurrencies that you can earn more of more quickly. As mentioned early, Genesis mining allows individuals to receive a payout in Bitcoin through different altcoin mining contracts. So this means you can enter a Litecoin or an Ethereum contract and get paid in Bitcoin.

The other thing we'll discuss is how bitcoin has opened up the space for the growth of other cryptocurrencies.

Chapter 8: How Bitcoin Has Allowed Other Cryptocurrencies To Form

Anonymous

The first thing that Bitcoin did that some of the other cryptocurrencies didn't do is that it anonymizes everyone. You can have whatever password that you want and you can have whatever username that you want; the only thing that matters to Bitcoin is that it has your username and front and your key in the back. While a lot of cryptocurrencies do this, it isn't actually a common trait with all cryptocurrencies. There were some cryptocurrencies that required your real name or wanted to implement a system that could utilize your real name so that it could only be tied to you. By anonymizing the currency, the currency can't be tracked by anything other than the Bitcoin Network and the people who retain the ledgers. A good example of why this is important is because the government could buy a ton of Bitcoins and effectively control the market by only releasing Bitcoins at a pace that it believes is appropriate. If the government knew, like China might, that you were the individual that held a certain Bitcoin that it didn't have then it could request that you send the government the Bitcoin. By utilizing any type of username that you wanted, you effectively gain anonymization, which prevents government control over Bitcoins in side of its' own borders.

Peer2Peer Validations

Part 1 of decentralized control means that all the people who serve as noted in the Network's serve as validations of Bitcoins in the Network's. In other words, no transaction can go on inside of the Bitcoin Network where Bitcoin is utilized that isn't checked by thousands of other nodes that all have untampered with code. It's kind of like having an unlimited amount of notaries present for each and every transaction that occurs on the Bitcoin Network and this is far more powerful than any type of validation method used at a bank. In addition to this, due to the fact that the users of the Bitcoin networks are the Bitcoin users themselves this also means that there is no additional fee attached to validating transactions and keeping track of them. Essentially, it gets rid of the necessary jobs of a notary and a bookkeeper.

Decentralized Control

The second part of decentralized control is the fact that it is decentralized. This means that there is no one area that has more authoritative power over the economic system of Bitcoin and so no singular entity can control the influx or deflux of the system. This is very good for removing artificial bubbles that governments have created in the past with currency and so it creates a much more trusted Network amongst people who invest their time and money into the Bitcoin Network.

Controlled Release

This also means that there is a controlled release of Bitcoins rather than a fluctuating release like we've seen with much of the paper money currently in existence. Governments have blown up their amount of paper money being printed and this has caused governments like Greece to fall into a recession where there should not have been a recession in the first place. By having a controlled release base off of mathematical principles, every one can predict how the network will go in terms of growth and whether the network is dying or not.

Public Open Cryptology Methodology

The last part of this puzzle is the fact that the cryptology methodology involved with Bitcoin is open to the public for scrutiny. This means that other alternative coins are able to judge how Bitcoin handled the cryptology aspect of the coin and implement what it thinks is a better solution than Bitcoin.

All of these serve as a blueprint for each of the alternative coins that are currently out on the market and while those coins may have changed it slightly, this is the blueprint that's used for most of them. Since Bitcoin is so popular and so trusted but the value of Bitcoin and the Rarity of Bitcoin has gone up drastically, people have sought out ways to get access to other lesser-known cryptocurrencies so that it is not as difficult to farm them as Bitcoin currently is. The methodology of creating Bitcoin is easy to replicate and easy to change, but the access to Bitcoin has become more and more difficult, which means that the cap of Bitcoin is on the horizon. Even though there will be more Bitcoins to come out in the future, we cannot guarantee that we will have the technology to solve the blocks that are required on the Bitcoin Network and so alternative coins provide a option to switch over to a lesser-known network that isn't near its ending point. Additionally, because these lesser-known networks are easier to farm, people join in those networks so as to join what was effectively the Bitcoin rise in the beginning. Much of the people who are in the Bitcoin networks are people who found Bitcoin when it was small and wanted to explode it, now selling out as they reach thousands of dollars. Bitcoin was originally free for some users and as the value of

Bitcoin has gone up, people have wanted to get into the industry but the original people who were in the industry when Bitcoin was founded often payout so as to get the most amount of money that they possibly can and live a luxurious life. There are a lot of people who see the position that those people are in and want to be in those positions. All of these factors, the fact that Bitcoin is basically open to the public for recreation and redistribution as other names and the fact that it seems to be better when there are a lower amount of people help to increase the value that other coins have as Bitcoin seems to plateau.

Next, we will discuss another concept known as segwit.

Chapter 9: What is Segwit?

When you start looking at Bitcoin and Blockchain Technology, you'll start to notice there are actually a few different forms of Bitcoin. You might be wondering why these exist and which is real. There are multiple Bitcoin's, Bitcoin Cash and Bitcoin Gold and the 'normal' Bitcoin. To give you an idea of what the relationship is between the three Bitcoin's, we must need to understand what Segwit is.

Segwit, or Segregated Witness is the process by which the blockchain size of the network is increased. This is done through removing some transactions allowing faster and more transactions to occur. You can think of this like a memory card. The more full it is, the slower the memory card will be and the less memory can be held.

Soft fork vs Hard fork

So you might of heard this term before in cryptocurrencies, and if you haven't, that's okay, you'll hear it quite often. Soft forks and hard forks are exactly what it sounds like, a fork. It's essentially a brand out of the original network protocol. When the network requires a change, it goes through either one of these forks.

A soft fork is a *temporary* change to the system, an independent event occurring within the project. This is much like an update on the network.

A hard fork is a *permanent* change in the system and generally results in a creation of a new coin.

These forks occur due to divisions in the network, individuals' who want to support the current network and their goals, and individuals who want a change in the network. When the network requires a hard fork, this creates a 'new' coin, representing the 'new' project. You can see it like a pathway fork. If you're walking down the forest and you want to go to your friend's house, you'll take two different routes. Left allows you to go to friend A's house and right allows you to go to friend B's house. Whichever route you take will result in two different outcomes. This is essentially what hard forks are about, two sets of individuals with two different visions.

It's important to distinguish the fact that hard forks still use the same blockchain network. The only real different is the vision of the project.

Bitcoin Cash

Bitcoin Cash was released on the 1st August 2017. The community behind Bitcoin Cash (BCH) wanted to solve Bitcoin's scaling problem. Because Bitcoin only recently gained popularity, the network has yet to meet the high demand necessary for the cryptocurrency. This has led to major issues in the Bitcoin network, primarily slower transaction times and high fees. The excess demand for the original Bitcoin means that more transactions must go through a smaller blockchain. Considering miners get paid to process these transactions, they process transactions faster to those who are willing to pay more, making fees absolutely crazy. This is the grand issue that Bitcoin faces and Bitcoin Cash addresses this by working to increasing its block size (currently 8MB), roughly 8x faster than Bitcoin, allowing more transactions to go through.

Today, BTH is considered a direct rival to the original Bitcoin (BTC).

Bitcoin Gold

Much like BCH, the introduction of Bitcoin Gold was not at all welcoming. In fact, it came under more scrutiny than BCH.

Bitcoin Gold (BTG) focuses on the miners. It's goal is to improve the mining capabilities of Bitcoin mining by allowing more people to mine and reduce the amount of powerful machines to do the mining. This will allow even more decentralization to occur as anyone will be allowed to mine, opening up mining to a wider user base.

Conclusion

Congratulations! Welcome to the end of this book! You're now an expert in Bitcoin, and while this may be the end of this book, this is definitely not likely going to be all that you learn about Bitcoin. Due to the ever-increasing Rarity of Bitcoin, there are likely to be several different markets that pop up so that the Rarity of Bitcoin doesn't begin to exclude other members from the Bitcoin community. There are currently 16 million Bitcoins on the market and there are only ever supposed to be 21 million. This means it's really important for the community to get together and collaborate on what to do so that Bitcoin doesn't end as fast as many people see it ending.

I hope you received valuable from this book, if you enjoyed this book, please leave a review on Amazon.com. Any review is greatly appreciated and I would like to thank you again for choosing this book. I strive to do the best I can and constantly revise the content.

Mastering Ethereum: The Ultimate Guide for Beginners to Understanding Ethereum Technology, Ethereum Investing, Ethereum Mining and Other Cryptocurrencies.

Introduction

I want to thank you for choosing and purchasing this book, *'Mastering Ethereum: The Ultimate Guide for Beginners to Understanding Ethereum Technology, Ethereum Investing, Ethereum Mining and Other Cryptocurrencies."* In this book you'll find everything you need to know about Ethereum, from the history of Ethereum, to the nitty gritty side of Ethereum Mining. This book will be your ultimate guide and something you can refer to now, and also in the future. As a BONUS, not only is this book about the essentials of Ethereum, information about other Cryptocurrencies will be added for your benefit.

If you're new to Cryptocurrencies, you may be wondering what on earth is the term 'Ethereum'? I myself was curious too. I wondered if it was some sort of new sci-fi movie that was released or an extension of the never ending Transformers saga. In some ways it could be, but that we will have to wait. In this present day, Ethereum is a new age revolution, being the second biggest cryptocurrency after Bitcoin. It has made headlines all around the world being the leader in alternative coins, allowing itself to explode in value in 2017. If you're familiar with cryptocurrencies, the term 'Ethereum', is just another text book, day-to-day word we all use. I myself started investing into cryptocurrencies with Ethereum, and if you've read my previous book, 'Mastering Bitcoin', you'd know I started investing because of my friend. Not only did he make an outstanding 400% return on his investment, he told me his next investment project was Ethereum. I was curious to know what this was and I studied everything I could about Ethereum, and here we are.

I know you are excited to learn about Ethereum, and we'll get started in a second. Again, I'd like to thank you for choosing this book. I have comprised everything I know about Ethereum in my years of experience, and I know you'll enjoy this book. This is the beginning of your cryptocurrency adventure and I hope you're as excited as I am. Let's get started!

Chapter 1: History of Ethereum

A Brief History on Ethereum

Ethereum was originally proposed in late 2013 with the initial release of its white paper by Russian-born Canadian, Vitalik Buterin. Buterin was not satisfied with the nature of Bitcoin. It would be too complex to change and this formed his desire to create a new platform instead, named Ethereum. During prior release, in 2014, there was an online sale that pushed the Ethereum coin into the market, however it wasn't until mid 2015, roughly one and half years later after the initial release of the white paper, when the Ethereum project officially went live and running. Due the dozens, if not hundreds of developers, engineers and scientists that were working on the project, Ethereum exceeded expectations, resulting in a rapid expansion. This allowed Ethereum to release projects frequently and has allowed Ethereum to become the second biggest cryptocurrency today (as of October 2017)

What is a Cryptocurrency?

Cryptocurrency is a coined terminology that primarily deals with a bit of encrypted text that represents a value in a market. The way a cryptocurrency normally works is that you have a username (known as an address) that represents your identity in the cryptocurrency network and you also have a small bit of encrypted text that comes after your username that represents the actual coin that is in your possession. Whenever you trade that coin, the username is switched but the encrypted text stays the same. Since the text is encrypted with a very powerful encryption system, this makes the coin very rare and thus creates value in the coin.

What does it mean to be Decentralized?

To understand this, let's go ahead and go over how money has actually evolved over time. In the beginning, it was not even money that allowed us to exchange things. During the beginning of civilization, we primarily traded items rather than money and this was because not a lot of people had the same resource. However, as populations expanded and resource manipulation expanded, those resources became duplicative and the market had the problem of mismatch in product demands. This essentially was a case where somebody had something that was similar to a lamb or a fruit and they tried to trade it to somebody who had plenty of lambs or fruits. This created a massive problem due to the fact that if you couldn't trade for the items that you needed then you would easily just spiral down into what would essentially be stone-age poverty. Then someone had the bright idea to take items and turn that into gold. Gold represented a standard and it also represented the worth of an item. The rarity of gold allowed it to be utilized as the very first form of coin monetization. Having said that, gold actually wasn't the first because they didn't really know how to transform gold just yet and so the very first one was copper because of how common it was. People were able to trade this this type of currency whenever they wanted to but as copper became less and less rare, its' value begin to drop drastically and so this is when silver came into the picture. The same thing happened to silver until gold came into the picture. The same thing happened to gold and nothing changed.

Essentially, we are all kept agreeing on the gold value. Gold has been the primary monetary value in the marketplace for the past 2000 years until somebody had the bright idea to change physical, rare metals into paper representation of those metals. This is what we know as the gold standard. This meant that for every dollar, there was a specific dollar amount that would equal a specific gold amount. While I may be talking about dollars, this was the representation of most of the money in the world. The problem is that money is limited and if you really want to make a good amount of money, you can't really make that money if someone has all that money in the first place. Establishing a gold standard basically put a cap limit on how much a person can progress. Therefore, the gold standard was changed into what we know as Fiat money. Fiat money is known as a type of money that is symbolic in nature. You put your worth on the dollar bill. If no one actually saw value in the dollar bill because it is Fiat money, the dollar bill would no longer be worth anything. This has been the standard for the past hundred years.

Then in 2009, we came out with cryptocurrency. However, there's a special component of Fiat money that you need to understand before we delve into cryptocurrency. You see, for the dollar, the money is actually printed by one organization that is controlled by a private bank known as the Federal Reserve. This private bank chooses how much to print each year so that money continues to be a useful item in our society. Over time, this printed amount becomes unmanageable in cases that you can see such as Greece falling or Japan falling. Essentially, there is so much paper money in the works that it becomes pennies rather than dollars and so no one wants to work with it. The only way that anyone has saved themselves from these pennies is to go to a new Fiat money. For the longest time the American dollar has held the gold standard when it comes to Fiat money. Everybody thought it would be a good idea to place their trust in America because of how big and powerful it was in the financial and military realm. The problem is that America as a whole is a good country but the corporations that control the vast majority of the wealth are generally not that intelligent. During 2008, we suffered the biggest recession that we've seen since the Great Depression. The American dollar has been losing value ever since and since the biggest loaner to America is China, China doesn't want to be caught in a situation where the debtor cannot pay his debt. This brings us to cryptocurrency, which is a new form of Fiat money but at a finite amount. You see, there is no one that can tell the Bitcoin or the Ethereum to print more. Bitcoin and Ethereum simply print as much as they are programmed to print and they don't even print it, they just digitally create the numbers in the monetary spheres that is Bitcoin and Ethereum . Decentralization means that there is no one company that controls the vast majority of how Bitcoin or Ethereum is produced and so since there is no one controlling this massive cryptocurrency, there is no central governing body. Everybody checks everybody and it is a mixture of the days when we used to trade each other with actual items and Fiat money. For many, this is seen as the evolution of money.

What is an Altcoin?

Normally when somebody refers to an Altcoin they are actually referring to an alternative cryptocurrency coin that is not Bitcoin. Bitcoin represents the beginning of the cryptocurrency trend and so it's usually referred to as the original cryptocurrency coin but the truth is the Bitcoin really isn't the first cryptocurrency, it's just the first cryptocurrency coin that became popular. Alternative cryptocurrency represents a market of cryptocurrencies rather than a specific individual cryptocurrency. People refer to them as alternative cryptocurrency coins otherwise known as Altcoins simply because it came after Bitcoin.

Ethereum vs. Ethereum Classic

The Ethereum blockchain is written in C++, Go, and Rust, which are all very powerful and very quick languages. The best part is that it was written for x86 systems and ARM platforms so it will not be going away for a long time. However, the system was closed off in its own little environment for a very long time and it was not public, and so in 2015, around 12 million coins flooded the market for sales, and ever since then it's been a crazy ride. Now, Ethereum has experienced some problems and this has resulted in two different Ethereum, Ethereum and Ethereum Classic. You might be wondering where in the world do Ethereum and Ethereum classic come from and how do they differentiate. Well, there was a project called the DAO, which was a way of formalizing contracts as a way of transactions in businesses. The problem is that because of security issues, this project failed and the result of this issue actually ended up creating a divergent point between the two different cryptocurrencies. This created a 'hardfork' which is essentially a split in the Blockchain, resulting in the two Ethereum today. So they are technically both Ethereum but Ethereum Classic follows an older pattern while the Ethereum you know today has a little bit more security add to do it.

Chapter 2: How Cryptocurrency Works?

What is an Ether Blockchain

A blockchain is known as the Ledger of whatever cryptocurrency that you're talking about because it keeps all of the records of all the transactions that have ever happened as well as all of the current coins in rotation. This is a linked list of hashed pointers that keep a timestamp of the current transaction along with the transaction data required to make the transaction. This blockchain is then distributed amongst everyone in the cryptocurrency network so that they can double-check any transaction that is currently taking place. An 'Ether' is simply the token of the Ethereum blockchain. The Ether token is used within this network to run operations, much like money in day-to-day society, Ether is essentially money of the Ethereum network. It is also known as 'ETH' in cryptocurrency markets.

Free Beginnings

When a cryptocurrency first lands on the market, it's usually free and this is because the only usual way to get it around to people is to make it free. People are not going to simply invest their time and money in something that's literally worth nothing. However, once people actually own it and they begin to play around with it, these currencies begin to gain attraction and therefore gain value. However, we see a very clear trend with most cryptocurrencies that they start out free so that people can test them and to see how reliable they are and then the market begins to accept it. This actually happened with Bitcoin where a vast majority of the beginning users received free Bitcoins as a result of doing something that the developers of Bitcoin wanted them to do. The actual value of Bitcoin didn't rise until much later in the Bitcoin life cycle as it stands right now.

Market Rarity Equals Value

However, once the market actually gets the coins, the value of that coin begins to rise because people have it and other people don't. This is true about every type of currency that has ever existed. Gold was really something that only the rich had during the medieval times simply because of how rare the gold was while the everyday peasant had a copper coin that they could utilize in the markets. Once the coin got onto the market, the value of the coin began to increase but the coins value is based on how rare the coin actually is so if you can begin to control the rarity of the coin then you can actually control the value of the coin itself. However, cryptocurrencies provide a different form of rarity. You see, previous monetization values such as gold and copper became rare because their existence was rare. Cryptocurrency becomes rare because the more people that join in the game of mining cryptocurrency the harder it is to mine those cryptocurrencies. Therefore, you need more and more power in order to get those cryptocurrencies and only those with the most amount of power get the most amount of cryptocurrencies. This process increases the rarity of the cryptocurrency and this in turn raises the value of the cryptocurrency. You can think of this process much like *deflation*, the less there is, the rarer it is.

Releasing Coins Decreases Value

Every time coins are released into the market, the value of those coins temporarily goes down because the coins represented a certain value before those coins got released and then the value goes down because there's more coins in the market. This is a very temporary bend in the value of the coin because once the coins have been released into the market, then everyone has to mine for more coins out of more difficult rates and this is what increases the overall value of the cryptocurrency. You can think of this process much like *inflation*, the more there is, the less rare it is.

Proof of Work Increases Market Value

As I already mentioned before, the market value of cryptocurrency is based on how difficult it is to mine for these coins. This is done by the concept of proof of work. Previously, digital currencies had no ways of proving that they were the original copy simply because you were capable of copying and pasting all sorts of documents because they're digital. This was known as the double spending law but if you have a ledger that keeps all of the transactions that have happened including the mining of new currencies, then you have the ability to stop double spending. Essentially, you have the market that is using those currencies, and those mining for currencies. The miners check for the validations of those transactions so that if a currency tries to double spend, the market that actually uses that currency double-checks who actually has that currency and if the person who currently has the currency is not the person that is trading over the currency, the market rejects the transaction. This is known as the proof-of-work concept and it's also how cryptocurrency mining actually occurs. You are simply checking to make sure that everybody is making appropriate transactions in the network and when the network wants to make a transaction check, it sends out the check amongst everyone in the network and the first one to figure it out gets a small package of coins but the network shares those coins amongst all the computers that served to figure out the encryption puzzle to check if the appropriate transaction took place. We know this as the blockchain. The Ethereum platform has been based off of the same proof-of-work concept that Bitcoin was based off but now they are attempting to make the move to proof of stake, which allows for the use of virtual mining.

To Come: Proof of Stake

The problem with proof of work is that it consumes massive amounts of energy, as shown when we dive into actually mining coins ourselves later on in this book. Eventually, they will reach a point where there are no more Bitcoins to provide the people who are known as cryptocurrency miners with the rewards they currently treasure. At that time, the value of Bitcoin is pretty much determined by the transaction fees that go along with any transactions on the Bitcoin Network. Since this doesn't really require the Goliath sized workload of the cryptocurrency Farms that are out there, there's no real reason for miners to not just accept every transaction fee that any person creates. This means that the transaction fee will go down and the lack of money making possibilities will cause miners to simply disappear from the network. On the other hand, Ethereum provides a different way of earning these coins and that is to say that you have a certain amount of stake inside of Ethereum. Essentially, the miners of Ethereum will also run out of coins to mine but in order to reward miners of Ethereum, those that have the most amount of coins can then mine the most amount of coins. In other words, if you managed to obtain 2% of all the Ethereum that's on the network then you are also allowed to mine 2% of all the Ethereum on the network. This allows individuals to continuously build up their resources without sacrificing the hardware that Bitcoin chomps on. Instead, it's about who can perform the most amount of transactions now but, to make it fair, the system randomizes the choice of who gets to mine. This is because the calculation for how many Ethereum coins an individual has is a very easy calculation for the network to provide as a way of validation. The network keeps track of how many coins a certain account has and if you have the same amount of coins as listed in the account, it serves as a validation but if you have less you get less of a reward. It's a very easy way of calculating for the purpose of validation but there are quite a few problems with it and there may be more problems to come so since the actual concept hasn't been implemented in Ethereum just yet, we will let the future decide what problems will come of this.

Chapter 3: Smart Contracts

What is a Smart Contract?

All right, so the coolest thing about Ethereum is the ability to utilize smart contracts but a lot of people get confused between a regular contract and a smart contract. However, let's talk about this in the form of automobiles because a lot of people know how to purchase an automobile and if you're reading this book, the odds that you've purchased an automobile is pretty high. In this process, you first go to a notable dealership or used car salesman and you inspect the product beforehand, then you talk it out and determine which is the best price for you before you go to the bank and request money out of your bank. Your bank then utilizes a safety system known as a certified check or a direct check that the bank personally takes responsibility for and then provides you that money. This money is then taken to the dealership where the individual who is selling the car now begins the process of giving you the car. Both you and the dealership or the used cars salesman is in a long drawn-out process of filling out information so that all of the information can be deposited to the DMV. This DMV serves as a giant file bucket to verify who owns what cars and when they obtained them. Once the DMV approves your car, you then have to register your car to the DMV so that they can up keep the cost of holding those files. Meanwhile, you have to take the car home and apply things like insurance and that is the end of the chain for buying a car. If you notice, this process was actually slowed down due to two major things. The first thing is that your bank needed to give you a way to secure the amount of money that is on a check because a personal check could be bounced and the bank knows that the person selling you the car needs a check that is the value that they are wanting. Therefore, they created the system called a secure check, which allows the person selling the item to rely on the bank's reputation rather than the individual buying the car to back the money up. Then, a file is needed to be kept so that the dealership couldn't just say "oh he never bought that car" and just take the car back even though he got the money. He could easily say that the money was just given to him out of being a nice stranger although I highly doubt that that is something that would happen. However, there is still that possibility so what the DMV needs to do is it needs to register who actually owns the car, when they bought it and keep all the different details on the car. These two processes took a system that would normally take maybe a day to complete and turned it into nearly a week or more depending on how difficult your system that you have to deal with is.

That was a standard contract and this new contract, otherwise known as a smart contract, is different and better. The smart contract is built on to the blockchain that makes Ethereum worth investing and why it's a cryptocurrency. This automatically makes the contract trustworthy. The cryptocurrency itself is a trusted form of money and you can't just make up the amount of money that you have in cryptocurrency so the money is its own secure check. Since the information on the car could easily be uploaded to the blockchain for further information of who owned the car and the details of the car, you no longer need the DMV. Essentially, you would go and look at a car to where you would want to buy it and you would be able to buy it on the spot whether it is online or offline. You see, in this chain you would go find the car that you wanted that was attached to the blockchain and then you would transfer the Ethereum from your account into the blockchain and if it met the amount that the dealer was asking for then the car would be given to you.

Since the money is trusted and the information in the blockchain is trusted, there is no need for these middlemen called the bank and the DMV. The best part about this is the reason why most cars are not sold online is due to the fact that you have to deal with your local DMV and bank and so most places build a giant shop and take up land just because we have to deal with these middlemen. Instead of dealing with these organizations, we can bring the car industry into the online space and we can begin exchanging these cars like the products that we should have been exchanging them long before we started exchanging things like toothpaste on Amazon and voltmeters on eBay. This is the power of a smart contract and this is the difference between a smart contract and a regular contract.

The First Design

The first design or rather the first concept of a smart contract actually developed in 1996 by Nick's Szabo. The idea that he created was actually that the smart contract would be utilized for a much wider spectrum that could be defined with very specific boundaries created by logic and would eventually be enforced through the protocols created by cryptography. The problem is that these smart contracts were really the idea of how you could further the process of creating the computations needed in order to maintain the blockchain itself. The actual idea as we know of it right now is not one where individuals are capable of making online transactions that remove middlemen but more of the idea of how to maintain the validity of a blockchain. The first popular form of a smart contract was actually known as DAO and this was for a venture capital funding campaign that was currently running on Ethereum but then the ironic part about this is that the platform was hacked and all the Ethereum was drained in literally less than a month.

The Implementations that Followed

While Ethereum is the most widely used cryptocurrency when it comes to Smart contracts, there are actually others that have utilized this technology. For instance, RootStock is a powerful platform that is derived off of the Bitcoin blockchain that acts as a smart contract platform but this technology, of course, works with Ethereum as well. Then you have cryptocurrencies like Burstcoin and Qora, which utilize the notion of automated transactions but these are not the general purpose ideas that we think of whenever we think of smart contracts with Ethereum.

The Flaws in Smart Contracts

Now as much as smart contracts seem like they are the cars of tomorrow, they are built off of code and code usually has bugs in it. If the actual code itself doesn't have bugs in it then the virtual machine that runs it has bugs, the compiler itself may have bugs, the network blockchain can be DDOSed into submitting to a certain will, the bugs (on the network, if they are found) will be slow to repair, and there are a lot of problems with smart contracts. A lot of people like to act like this is the Holy Grail of all contracts but due to the flaws of programmatic error, we have so many bugs that could happen that it is actually somewhat difficult to fully trust a smart contract. Until the system is designed so that it is nearly agreed to be perfect, smart contracts are not likely to enter any markets where government backing or medical industry guarantees are capable of carrying out those guarantees without fear of the system being the problem.

What do Gas and Ether mean in the Ethereum Environment?

Whenever there is a transaction on the Ethereum environment, there has to be an operational task that is meant to validate and verify both sides of the exchanging parties currencies so that the Ethereum network avoids the double spending problem. As odd as it may seem, you actually spend Ether in the Ethereum environment and you get Ether coins in exchange for mining them. However, if you were to transfer them to a person then you would be charged a Gas fee (Gas is the internal pricing for running a transaction or contract in the Ethereum network). Gas fees are non-refundable to either party and the system automatically converts the Ether into Gas in order to pay for the fee for the operational costs it took to run the transaction. This Gas is then distributed amongst the Ethereum network as rewards for continuously perpetuating the Ethereum network. This is very different from Bitcoin because Bitcoin actually has a set limit on how much cryptocurrency is going to come out in the future to the point of 21 million whereas Ethereum was built with the limitation in mind and so whenever a transaction occurs, a little bit of that transaction goes back into the environment and since transactions are happening all the time a ton of Ethereum is going back into the Ethereum environment.

What is an Oracle?

Now when I said that smart contracts have the potential to remove the middlemen that we have to deal with, that isn't entirely true because smart contracts are not as capable as they're made out to be. You see, smart contracts do have the capabilities of securing data on the network so that a transaction is cleared much like the way I described. The problem is that that information has no way to actually get into the network and this is where something called an Oracle comes in. An Oracle serves as the middleman for the cryptocurrency coin and the cryptocurrency blockchain. Essentially, it allows the individuals on the network to develop an API that gives the financial individuals that want to work with smart contracts the ability to interact with this smart contract technology. Therefore, Oracles are probably one of the more annoying problems that we're going to have to deal with because the smart contracts on the network are not all that good by default. Essentially, we have to do what HTML did for the World Wide Web. The World Wide Web was originally just text based files and there were no real way to look at a web page. Essentially, the world wide web looked like a giant file system. Therefore, somebody came along and developed HTML and you see where that ended up.

What is Timestamping?

A timestamp, in the digital sense, represents the time at which something occurred and it acts as a stamp because it records that time and only that time. This is very simpler to think of if you were to think of an accountant in keeping transactions of when certain transactions occurred. The only difference between the timestamp that the accountant uses and the timestamp that the computer uses is that the computer will usually record down to the smallest possible version of time that you can possibly conceive of so as to get a very accurate description of exactly when that happened. Therefore, an accountant would say that something happened at 3:45, but a computer would say that it happened at 3, 45 minutes from 3, and 21 nanoseconds from 45 minutes. In other words it would look something like this: 3:45:0000029.As you can see, you can get far more precise transaction times and normally transactions will not happen at the exact same nanosecond so the validity of the system is very reliable. The Bitcoin currency system or rather the cryptocurrency system is not the first type of program that utilizes this timestamp because whenever you do anything with credit cards, anything with practically all the different social media applications, and even your phone application, they all use this version of timestamp because it accurately records when things happened so that they can put it in the proper order.

Chapter 4: The Potential of Ethereum

The Latency of Ethereum

The process in which Ethereum checks for the validation of transactions is actually faster than that of Bitcoin which means that there can be a lot more transactions occurring than with Bitcoin. Additionally, the Ethereum actually utilizes more nodes than Bitcoin so it is more security proof so not only is it faster in this case but it is also providing the additional benefit of being more robust in its' security.

Why Ethereum is a Long-Term Investment?

The core concepts behind these two cryptocurrencies are practically the same but the reason why Ethereum is seen as a long-term investment is primarily due to the giant corporations that have taken a look at Ethereum. The core concept of smart contracts is the reason why Ethereum is currently the long-term investment for most individuals because Bitcoin doesn't have a competing technology for this and smart contracts are a vital part of an ecosystem built off of money. In other words, the smart contract allows individuals to begin replacing jobs and increasing the validation for transactions while Bitcoin just doesn't do that. This is why Ethereum is seen as the long-term investment of these two cryptocurrencies.

The Legality of Ethereum?

The legality of Ethereum is very similar to the legality of Bitcoin but the problem with Ethereum is the smart contract itself. If these smart contracts come in to replace contracts then it removes so many jobs that it is mind-blowing. There are so many jobs that are built in place simply to validate transactions because you have the DMV, which is utilized to validate transactions with cars and sometimes tickets. You have The Mailing Service, which is utilized to validate that a package has arrived either through digital format or physical format and one person could literally do the job of this validation so instead of the one person collecting all the packages information and ensuring that it was sent out that morning, you have Ethereum just keeping track of whether the item was delivered at the door or not. You have Banks period. Banks are the ones that would literally topple over if this became the mainstream thing. Banks would actually be seen as odd. The reason being is because a bank is simply there to hold onto money so that you can either spend it in paper form or digital form. The rest of a bank's job is validation. You have to validate that you have the money in the account, you have to validate that you have the ability to take out that loan, you have to validate almost everything you do with a bank account but with Ethereum it is automatically validated. Therefore, if it isn't illegal now, banks will attempt to lobby to get it to be illegal because they would literally die as a business if it became the standard.

Why Ethereum won't be the Last Altcoin

The reason why there are many alternative cryptocurrency coins in the first place is because people found better ways to do stuff. This won't be the first and won't be the last, well I know it obviously won't be the first but it will not definitely be the last. If there is anything to learn from the current alternative cryptocurrencies out there and the top dog of them all right now, which is Bitcoin, people just keep on creating different cryptocurrencies simply because they want to make the best one that everybody wants to invest in and this means that until someone comes on top with all the neat features and little gadgets that we want, there will never be a last alternative currency.

Chapter 5: Storing Ethereum Coins

Hard Storage

Just like Bitcoin, there are a few ways to store Ethereum coins and the truth of the matter is that there are really only three ways to store these alternative coins. The first, primary method, is to store the coin on a more permanent type of platform. The first method of hard storage is to simply store it on the hard drive that you do your mining and you're investing on, which is what most beginners begin to store their hard earned Ethereum coins on so that it's just the easiest method possible. For this, you're handed a digital wallet that can keep track of those coins along with any other transactions that you might have had on the same network.

The more security-conscious individuals that have gathered quite a bit more Ethereum coins often try to store these coins on medium storages such as a USB stick or an SD card. The reason why this is more security conscious is because a USB stick or an SD card can be hidden throughout the house without being attached to a very big and identifying computer source. This means that it's much harder to steal the USB stick or SD card in this case but the added bonus is that if your computer gets infected with a ransomware virus or any type of key logger, the individual will only ever have access to those digital keys to the coins if they happen to have the virus on at the same time that you plug the device into the computer rather than 24 hours of the day. This is if you haven't been able to figure out where their virus is and haven't removed it from your computer because at this level, these things become more prominent to your view and so you keep up with the maintenance on your computer so as to keep it safe. The most popular and recommended cryptocurrency USB hard drive is the Ledger Nano S.

For more information, visit wonpublications.com/ledger

There are a few problems with these types of storage mediums because these types of storage mediums are known for being somewhat volatile by nature. If you whack a USB against a hard surface for a very long time there is a very high chance that all of the data is completely wiped from the USB stick or the data becomes corrupt and this is the truth of the SD card as well because these two platforms are very volatile. A less volatile platform would be that of an Solid State Storage Drive, otherwise known as an SSD. This type of Drive is very durable and very quick whenever writing information to it so you wouldn't need to keep it connected to the computer for very long but they are significantly more expensive than their counterparts of storage. There is also the potential that you can lose your hard wallet. Most people keep their USB's on their house keychains or car keychains for protection, but in the chance you lose it, it's impossible to get the data back.

Paper Storage

The second method of storing your Ethereum coins Is to simply create a paper that controls all of the digits that you have and this is normally referred to as the paper money of cryptocurrency. The reason why paper money is utilize is because not only is it very difficult to grab all the keys at once, unlike the digital platforms of both the USB stick or the SSD but it is also rather difficult to physically steal all of your paper notes. For example, you don't need all of your paper notes should you leave the house and so a person who doesn't understand cryptocurrency would not understand the value behind a stack of papers with random digits on it. Imagine if you were a burglar and you had no idea of cryptocurrency and so when you saw that a victim had a stack of pieces of paper with ciphers on them, what exactly would you think at that point? This form of currency is widely used by the heavily secure conscious people but it does come with the added problem of having to manually enter any of the keys that you stored on paper. This means that transactions could take considerably longer than they would normally take if you had a digital wallet and you would have to wipe your drive free of the coins on your account in order for the paper money to actually mean anything. Needless to say, this is really only utilized by individuals who intend to take their paper money with them to a specific spot where they are going to hand over the bill of cryptocurrency to a vendor or they simply want to be more security conscious of their money.

Cloud Storage

Cloud storage is the third and final form of storing your Ethereum coins and this refers to either having a website where you store your Ethereum coins like you would on a regular hard drive or where it is an online wallet that allows you to do transactions. There are risks with either of these options. With a cloud storage medium, you run into the risk of anyone gaining access to the password of your cloud storage device or if the cloud storage service itself becomes a target of being hacked where all the information of the customers are stolen. Additionally, with both of the services you run into the risk of an employee having access to your account and seeing a giant amount of Ethereum coins being stored on your cloud storage. If they were very good at what they did in their IT job then they could simply steal the coins and make it look like it was never there in the first place. The problem with an online wallet is that there are no real trusted organizations at this point that will hold your Ethereum coins in an online wallet and so you run into the risk where if you want to do this method, you need to understand that the owner of this wallet could easily just take all the coins that you saved up inside of that wallet. This has actually happened more than once and many people have lost thousands of cryptocurrency due to these shady individuals. In fact, these shady individuals are generally the reason why most people simply don't even look out the cloud storage possibility of storing their cryptocurrency. Having said that, cloud storage is also the easiest form of storing these digital forms of cryptocurrency because you can generally access these drives from anywhere that you wanted to such as inside of a crypto-currency bar or on the streets with your cell phone plan. Needless to say, a lot of people like to store small bits of their cryptocurrency on their online drives so as to have immediate access to it if they want to buy something in their cryptocurrency.

There are many pros and cons to all types of storages. Personally I'm not a big user of hard wallets, but I know some individuals love and are reliable with hard ware devices. An alternative method would be diversifying all of these. I know some people like to have some on their Ledger Nano S and some on an online wallet. It is completely up to you.

Chapter 6: Trading in Ethereum

Paper for Digital

The first thing that you can do with a cryptocurrency is actually switch it from a cryptocurrency back to the Fiat money that is more usable in Daily applications. Most people think that these applications for cryptocurrency are very small and very dense so they don't want to fully invest into the cryptocurrency market but rather get the rewards from the cryptocurrency market that they would receive if they turned their hard-earned cryptocurrency into cash. For instance, if you manage to grab a Bitcoin for the day then you would easily have thousands of dollars because Bitcoins are currently worth thousands of dollars per Bitcoin. However, the common use for the cryptocurrency is to just let it save up and then once it becomes something that you can utilize, you either go through a digital currency exchange like BitPay, where you can change your Bitcoins or your alternative coins into actual Fiat money. This is a very flexible way to work with the money but at the same time there are some issues that come up with the worth of a Bitcoin if you are too slow to do this or you are too quick to do this.

Digital for Digital

A less common trend amongst the average individual who just does mining for cryptocurrency for fun, but an equally common trend amongst investors who treat cryptocurrency like it's a stock trade is the fact that you can trade cryptocurrency for cryptocurrency. Therefore, if you earn a certain portion of Ethereum as it is right now and then trade that Ethereum for Ethereum Classic because you might think it will do better then you can go on to a market for that and trade for cryptocurrencies. The idea behind this is that certain cryptocurrencies rise in value faster than others and so what ends up happening is that people want to earn a cryptocurrency that's popular right now but also want to trade it for something that they think is on the rise and will rise quicker than the one they are earning. This may not make sense for a lot of people but the honest truth about it is that if you have something that's worth more value than the item that you want but the item that you want is going to have more value in the future, then it makes sense to not spend time working on the one that you want if it is easier to work on the one that you have. This is the concept of trading digital currency with other digital currency.

Performing Work for Ethereum

As odd as it may seem, many people are willing to work for alternate cryptocurrencies because of the worth of the cryptocurrency at the time. In fact, there are websites that are specifically dedicated to offering job positions based off of Bitcoin. Even a company like Fiverr has joined the mix by offering an option to pay out in Bitcoin. This is because Bitcoin removes the barriers Because alternate current cryptocurrencies are based on the Bitcoin model, they also happen to remove the barrier to many of the problems that come with Fiat money. Fiat money has to go through a middleman, which we all know as a bank, but Banks often come with transaction fees, wire transfer fees, and foreign or national fees that end up piling on top of other fees to make the transaction almost a nightmare for anything that is of a small size. If you are just trying to switch over a currency for a few hundred dollars then you don't want to pay nearly $60 in fees just so that you can do that and so these alternate cryptocurrencies allow you to make that exchange. Additionally, most of the time you can just trade in your Bitcoin or your alternate currency into a system like BitPay where you deposit the amount of money that you want with a fee from BitPay for doing the service for you into your account directly rather than trying to use the bank's system of converting money. A good example of why I would use Bitcoin is if I were to have another customer from Australia because when I got paid through PayPal with Australian money, the exchange rate was absolutely horrible and I actually lost $60 on a $300 invoice. That is nearly one-fifth of the money that I made that went into a conversion fee just because PayPal needed that money to correct the value difference between the two currencies. I would go through a service like BitPay where I might pay a 5% or 10% fee in an exchange so that I can change that Australian dollars into United States dollars. This is actually one of the most common practices for an application inside of the cryptocurrency environment but it's not the only form of work that can be paid with cryptocurrency. The other form of work is actually at convenience stores or restaurants because there are locations that are specifically designed so that they can accept Bitcoin as payment. In these places you use Bitcoin as regular money and you simply just hand them your address where they transfer the necessary amount of Bitcoins from your address and to their address. This makes the process of having to deal with any Fiat money virtually non-existent and some owners of buildings actually accept a form of currency in the cryptocurrency market because they know that the value of that cryptocurrency is likely to go up so they see it as a loss for the person who is spending the money but also a gain on their part because whenever they accept the cryptocurrency they will be accepting a currency that will likely rise in value and so it will be worth more than it was originally when they accepted it.

Chapter 7: Ethereum as a Trade Market

Buy High Sell Short

There are four main ways to trade in side of the Ethereum Market and this really depends on what you want to do with it. You have to remember that the market for Ethereum is very similar to the trade market and so when you hear these terms, which are the titles of these paragraphs, they will be almost identical to the terms that are utilized inside of stock trading. Therefore, when you buy high and sell short, what it means is that you are waiting for the moment when the Ethereum looks like it's going to be worth less than what it's going to be worth in just 5 to 20 minutes down the road. Essentially, the idea is that if you manage to buy at a certain time, you can make a little bit of money back by waiting until the value of the product rises and this is actually generally how stock trade marketing is done in the first place the only difference is that this is Ethereum and cryptocurrencies are actually well known to be rather volatile so buying high and selling short is one of the most common practices when it comes to trading the product that is Ethereum.

Buy Low Sell Short

Now buying low and selling short is a lot less common due to the fact that Ethereum is rarely ever at a low point in the market. There are crashes in Ethereum and there are small Pockets where Ethereum might lose some value but the idea is that if you see the product losing value for maybe $0.20 for every single Ethereum going, you then buy because you know that there is going to be a rise because there's usually a rise. Performed in succession, you can usually come out on top by buying low and waiting a short bit for the price to come back up but you run the risk of buying during the time that a cryptocurrency is currently having a crash. The problem with this is that you spend a lot of money to buy these coins in the first place. Ethereum is approximately $300 in monetary USD value as of writing this book, and if I were to go and buy five of these coins, they would be the equivalent of $1,500 but if the market for Ethereum were to suddenly crash then I would have the problem of waiting until the price for Ethereum went back up over $1,500 before I ever made any money. Some people panic at this point because they believe that this Ethereum might not go back up but the proof is in the pudding that the cryptocurrencies usually go back up. These people panic and sell too early and wind up losing a little bit of money just so that they can stay safe and only lose a little bit of money. If the Ethereum doesn't come back up then they've lost that money and usually, when you're buying something like stocks, you don't buy in small quantities.

Buy Low Sell Long

Now this brings us to the other type of trade marketing and that is to simply buy it when it's low and wait a long time before you sell it. This actually makes sense for a lot of the alternative currencies because they've almost always started off slow and then a few years later they're at monstrously high peaks in terms of monetary value. Many of the individuals who may have amassed nearly a thousand Bitcoins cashed out once Bitcoin hit a certain thousand-dollar point. Well, if you have a thousand bitcoins that are worth a couple thousand dollars, you then have, basically, a million to 2 million dollars. This is the long game and it is considered the unwise decision when it comes to any type of stock trading at all. Most people prefer to sell short because it is easier to predict the market if you look at the market in small pictures rather than in very long strides. Usually, the only people who actually sell like this are individuals who are absolute fanatics at whatever they're buying.

Mine and Exchange

The last part of the stock exchange for Ethereum is to actually just feed the market because if you are a miner and you can produce the amount of Ethereum that you need to, you don't have to worry about the buying price of Ethereum until it falls. Most of your worrying, as a miner, is how much is the coin worth in terms of the voltage that you're utilizing in order to mine the coins. This final form is what ultimately drives the stock trade market for Ethereum because it introduces new coins into the mixture and creates the fluctuations of values that you see in the market that many of these players of the Ethereum Market play off of.

If you would like to learn a more in depth view on cryptocurrency, this is something I go into in my introductory book '*Cryptocurrency: 5 Expert Secrets for Beginners: Investing into Bitcoin, Ethereum and Litecoin.*',
Click the description below for more information,

https://www.amazon.com/dp/B07571MSY5

I've been investing for years and it's something I am truly passionate about. Since I started investing in cryptocurrencies, I've learnt a lot. I know as a beginner it can be extremely confusing, that's is why I dedicated my time to this series. If you're enjoying this book, please leave a review on Amazon.

Chapter 8: Mining Ethereum

What is CPU and GPU Mining?

To begin with the history of currency cryptocurrency mining, we first have to start with the CPU and this is because the CPU is where people first started figuring out how to solve these different blockchains. With most of the cryptocurrency mining that you do on a daily basis, you will still have access to CPU and GPU mining but certain pools are preventing the use of CPUs and GPUs. Essentially, the CPU would get a blockchain that it needed to figure out and this was okay because the CPU might have had a certain amount of cores but almost all of those cores usually ran anywhere from 2.5 to 4.0 gigahertz. This was when you started seeing a huge mountain of people purchasing CPU cores that were meant for servers because servers would be able to provide you with anywhere from 12 to 16 cores running at around 3 to 4 gigahertz. This was mind-blowingly fast at the time but the problem is that everything gets harder as more people get interested into cryptocurrency.

You can see why the industry of cryptocurrency switched from the CPU to the GPU. You see, the GPU is a fantastic little device if you can figure out how to use it because it is built for simple calculations and it has thousands of smaller cores that run in succession or parallel. These smaller cores allowed individuals to replicate the act of mining but at an explosively rapid rate. This has actually been the tradition for the past few years because people keep on buying the newest GPU on the market but the problem is that the GPU market wasn't quite ready for the influx of cryptocurrency miners and so this market has only really been dealing with gaming computers when it comes to these high-end GPUs. They don't mass produce these

GPUs on a level that the mining Community would purchase them at. For instance, one mining warehouse that is specifically dedicated to mining cryptocurrency will usually by anywhere from 300 to 400 GPUs. Now imagine that there are over four hundred companies buying GPUs in this amount and more. Needless to say, whenever a new GPU would hit the market, the market would essentially become devoid of that GPU because of the cryptocurrency miners. This has been the problem for the past year or so and so even though you can still utilize your CPU and GPU, don't expect to make the big bucks like you could have if you had invested in this around two to three years ago. Around that time, the hashes weren't that complex and the actual value of the coins were reasonable to the point where people were getting into the game just because they wanted to get into the game not because each coin represented thousands of dollars. Now that each coin represents thousands of dollars, everyone wants the new type of device that is specifically dedicated to cryptocurrency mining and this device allows individuals to go from the previous mega hashes that they used to experience with at least one GPU to a gigahash per device. We'll talk about why these different hash sizes are important in a little bit.

ASIC Mining

ASIC is the new device when it comes to cryptocurrency mining and it stands for Application-specific integrated-circuit. Therefore, it is specifically meant to perform cryptocurrency mining and this device usually costs the same amount of money that you would actually spend on a computer and that's because this is a very specialized device. These devices are extremely difficult to make for the public but they have almost always existed. In fact, Cisco is a proud owner of many of these types of devices but these devices that are coming out with cryptocurrency versions are not the same as the ones that Cisco provides. These devices are specifically built to only be used for the big bad boy otherwise known as Bitcoin mining. Due to this fact, many of the alternative coins are still utilizing CPU and GPU miners. Additionally, due to the fact that Bitcoin is so difficult to make money on without this device, many people are mining alternative coins in an attempt to actually make any money off of it.

Understanding The Market

The first thing that I have to cover is what the difference between a megahash and a gigahash. A megahash refers to how many megabytes can be transferred from the hash set in the blockchain and gigahash represents it in gigabytes. The faster that these two are the more money you can make but don't be fooled into thinking that you can just take your average GPU or CPU and generate some money off of it because there are a few things that you need to understand about the cost and benefit analysis before you even think that you're ready.

The first thing that you need to understand is the loss or rather the cost of electricity because that is the primary bill that you are going to be paying while trying to mine for the stuff. If you cannot cryptocurrency mine faster than your device causes electricity to be withdrawn then you are actually losing money and not making any money, which is why most people hit the newest GPUs on the market simply because those GPU cores are capable of providing the big hashset numbers that you need to make money while also doing it at a relatively low wattage amount. This allows individuals to build big gaming engines for computers and turns them into mining computers whenever they're out and about but they don't actually lose out because they process faster than they use electricity.

The other thing you need to pay attention to because the value of the coin really determines whether the benefit-cost analysis of your electricity in your house set really even matters. If your coin is super difficult to gather hash sets on then you are likely not going to make any money off of it. This is because the harder it is to gain hash sets the less money that your GPU or CPU is going to generate. If your coin doesn't actually represent a worth that represents its difficulty, then there is no sense in mining for it. Let's take my graphics card, which is an R9 270x. This is actually a graphics card that's really cheap and good for gaming. I haven't had to replace it ever since I bought it two years ago while it was Black Friday. I can still run some of the newest games in 60fps at 1080p because I just don't care about 4K. Having said that, my graphics card runs at about 8.9 megahashes. Now my electricity costs around $0.07 per thousands of watts per hour (KW/hr). Now, if you think that's impressive then you should sit back and wonder why I have such a graphics card because that graphics card would earn me a total of $4 a month. That's right, a graphics card that is capable of running some of the newest games at 60fps at 1080p will only earn me $4 a month while mining for Ethereum. This is because my graphics card is built for handling DirectX 11 based games and not the newest form of DirectX or even the Vulcan architecture that was recently developed by AMD. Therefore, while my graphics card is impressive, that doesn't mean squat in the cryptocurrency world because unless I have a very high core amount along with some very high processing amount, my graphics card is one of the weakest ones out there. That's not to say anything bad about my graphics card though because if you look at the new version of AMD Vega, which is a graphics card that costs nearly $500, it actually runs at about 40 megahashes. That is an improvement but it's nowhere near the amount that would justify running this thing 24/7 for an entire month because the estimated worth of what I would make off of that is just 45 bucks. Needless to say, you are going to need something like a GPU mining rig where you have close to ten to twenty of these AMD Vegas so that you can make any worthwhile money off of it.

The Ethereum Wallet

Now, something that's not really mentioned the whole lot in beginning cryptocurrency tutorials is that you need to have a wallet and that wallet is not well described. I'm going to break it down really simple for you so that you understand no matter how technically advanced you maybe. A wallet is just a software that keeps track of the specific hash algorithms you managed to solve in a network along with your username attached to it. It just keeps track of a long list of different encrypted text and that's it. Therefore, when they talk about a wallet in cryptocurrency what they are talking about is a software that keeps a long list of encrypted text in a text file with a very nice graphical user interface to make it easier to work with. Now my preferred wallet is actually Exodus because Exodus allows you to create multiple different wallets for multiple different currencies and if you are into farming a certain currency one day or a certain currency the next month. It doesn't matter, it will create a currency wallet for you and it's extremely easy to use.

Mining in Pools

The other part about this is that you will never be mining solo because you likely do not have the power to do this. Unless you are a millionaire or a billionaire reading this book, you are likely never going to have the power to solo mine or rather solar mine and outperform a pool mine. A pool mine or when people get together in a group and mine a specific part of the network means that all the CPU, GPU, and devices are coupled into one giant massive CPU that calculates the hash. This means that if the person in the pool has a GPU that can run a megahash at about 8.9 like I can and then there's also another person that can run a terrahash at about 10, then the person with the terahash is obviously going to solve the problem first but because I'm in the pool, I get to benefit from them solving the problem. It results in a much smaller portion of the coin that is released onto the market because the coin is split amongst everyone in a pool but at least I get some portion of the coin for the effort that I allowed my computer to take inside of figuring out the hatch. Therefore, it's almost always better to mine in pools rather than solo mine.

Getting Connected

So the first thing that you're going to want to do is download the wallet that I mentioned before because this is how I'm going to run this tutorial. Once you install this, you will be given an option to choose which coin you want to create a wallet for. After you create this wallet, you will have a right-hand menu where you can select additional wallets that you want to create. Whenever you create this wallet, it will generate an automatic wallet hash algorithm that you can then use as your identifying marker. This is normally placed below the receive and send button and above the calculated amount of coins you have of that currency. This will be known as your *whatever* currency address. Once you have downloaded that, you can then actually go to a website known as nanopool.org. This website has a long list of different alternative coins that you can mine utilizing the wallet that I just mentioned. Pick a currency version that you want to utilize and then click on the quick start button. Once you have clicked on the quick start button, you can receive a lot of useful information that you will not understand until you've been into cryptocurrency for a long time but the important part is that at the bottom of the page it will tell you how to actually connect to the mining resource for that cryptocurrency. Now this is the part that they don't tell you. Let's go ahead and cover how you would connect your mining resource once you've downloaded the Claymore DualMiner that is suggested on the website. So what you're downloading is a ZIP file and you're going to want to extract these files into a singular folder so that there are easy to locate. Once you've extracted them, you want to look through and you are either going to be editing a bat file or you are going to be editing a config file. For Ethereum, we are going to edit a bat file. You will recognize the file as start_only_eth.bat, which is something that you're going to right click on and click edit. This will open up notepad where you can then edit the information inside of the bat file. The bat file represents a command line executable so when you double click on it, it will run in the command line, which is something that you will need to tackle with your antivirus or your firewall. You are essentially looking for this line:

EthDcrMiner64.exe -epool eth-eu1.nanopool.org:9999 -ewal address/worker/email -epsw x -mode 1 -ftime 10

Now if you remember correctly, I told you where the address was for your wallet and where you see the address area after ewall, you will need to paste in the address to your wallet there. Then you will need to erase the worker default and apply your own name(what you feel like calling it). The final parameter is an option and you don't actually have to utilize it but it allows you to know when your worker is on or offline. Once you have edited this, you can then save it and close the notepad. Then you can double-click on the bat file and watch it go. Once it gets started up, it will tell you how fast it is figuring out the hatches and it will tell you how fast your hash rate is. From there you can actually determine whether your PC is capable of providing you with any money or not off of this venture. If not but if you want to continue it further, you're going to have to buy better GPUs because the current ASIC devices are primarily designed for Bitcoin only.

Conclusion

Congratulations! Welcome to the end of this book! You're now an expert in Ethereum, and while this may be the end of this book, this is definitely not likely going to be all that you learn about Ethereum. Vitalik Buterin is constantly working on expanding the Ethereum network and out of all the cryptocurrencies, Ethereum contains the largest potential. You can see this on the market, being the second largest cryptocurrency after Bitcoin. Keep your eyes on Ethereum, it is the one to watch in the upcoming years, and I personally am a true believer in the project.

I hope you received valuable from this book, if you enjoyed this book, please leave a review on Amazon.com. Any review is greatly appreciated and I would like to thank you again for choosing this book. I strive to do the best I can and constantly revise the content.

Blockchain: The Ultimate Guide to Understanding Blockchain Technology, Fintech, Bitcoin, and Other Cryptocurrencies.

Introduction

I want to thank you for choosing and purchasing this book, *'Blockchain: The Ultimate Guide to Understanding Blockchain Technology, Fintech, Bitcoin, and Other Cryptocurrencies.'* In this book you'll find everything you need to know about Blockchain, from the fundamentals of Blockchain Technology, to the nitty gritty side of Blockchain implications on industries. This book will be your ultimate guide and something you can refer to now, and also in the future. As a BONUS, not only is this book about the essentials of Blockchain Technology, information about other Cryptocurrencies will be added for your benefit.

Bitcoin, Ethereum, Litecoin... What do these cryptocurrencies have in common? Besides being a money magnet in modern investing, they're all based off the same technology. Not only these 3, but ALL cryptocurrencies are based off the Blockchain Technology. Blockchain Technology has come under mass adoption in recent years, with the growth of the famed Bitcoin, the blockchain has been implemented in different industries, primarily within Fintech, the financial industry. It has been used to track records, payments, processes, and today, you'll learn how one of the most underrated revolutions in technology is going to change our future.

I know you are excited to learn about the Blockchain, and we'll get started in a second. Again, I'd like to thank you for choosing this book. I have comprised everything I know about Blockchain in my years of experience, and I know you'll enjoy this book. This is the beginning of your cryptocurrency adventure and I hope you're as excited as I am. For more information, check out www.wonpublications.com. Let's get started!

Chapter 1: What is the Blockchain?

Before we get into depths of blockchain technology, we must understand what is the blockchain? The honest truth is that you can't really answer this question without telling you how blockchain works because blockchain is one of those few items that is explained through how it works rather than what it is. A lot of people consider it much like an accounting ledger, or for non-accountants, like a file cabinet full of files of information. However, the biggest difference is that it is online, and the fact that it is open source, meaning anyone can access the information at any given time.

How a List Works

To begin understanding blockchain, we first need to cover how we formulate a list, like a 'To-Do' list. Most of us will go through the items that we think we might need, or cover all of the items in our selected area. But let's say that the list we're going to work with within this first chapter is a grocery list. In a grocery list, you will either have the individual who will specifically think about what items are needed before they ever write the list and then they will check to make sure their assumptions are right.

The second individual will look over the different items in the fridge in comparison to an initial list that will instruct the writer of that list on what they should be checking in order to formulate a list upon what is missing.

In both cases, both individuals will need a prior list in which to check against in order to form a new list based off of the list that has been checked and insert anything that is missing into the new list. This is generally how a list works but in most programming languages this is not called a list, but an array. An array is a list of items that you first put into the list and in programming terms, we would form a first array that holds all the possible items that we want to check for inside of our fridge. Then we would develop a second array of all the items that are currently in our fridge. Finally, we would write a step-by-step process, otherwise known as an algorithm, to check the items in our first array to compare it to the items in the second array to create or generate a third array that will contain all the missing items inside of our fridge. This is how the computer views a list inside of the digitized world and so it is this first step that truly makes up the core logic of what blockchain is and, essentially, how it works.

How an Encrypted List Works

Let us first go over the first form of encryption that any encryption enthusiasts learn about whenever they begin studying encryption. This is known as the rotation 13 technique, and what it basically means is that you take a letter such as 'A' and you rotate through the alphabet until you get to the 13th place after what 'A' stands for. This, in our case, would be the letter 'M' because it comes 13 places after the letter 'A'. This is the most basic form of encryption on the planet and it was actually developed by Caesar, the emperor of Rome. The way that we would normally encrypt the list is pretty similar to this technique but we rely on the computer to develop a random system that will generate a random string of characters (a word), special characters such as an '!' or '?', numbers, and other such items that you can input via a keyboard. This computer-generated random string would essentially be what is known as our key.

Our key allows us to take the information in our list and encrypt it with an encryption technique that utilizes the random string and the numbers or letters inside of the word in the array to jumble the actual meaning of those words. The technique is usually far more advanced than rotation 13 but you can think of it as a technique that's usually very similar to how rotation 13 works but in a less predictable manner. Therefore, we have something known as a public key. This public key allows us to decrypt the information inside of the array. This is actually quite simple and very easy to understand. It's not really practical whenever you're trying to get users to interact with each other because you may have a public key, but that doesn't mean much if everybody else has a public key. If both individuals have public keys it essentially means they can see the same material that you are seeing. Keep in mind if no one else has your public key so no one else can see the material. This is when things get a little bit more complicated.

How a Shared Encrypted List Works

This is when we begin evolving our concept of the list into a much more complicated schema. When a shared list is encrypted, each individual is given a public key and the server has its own private key. The private key may be generated with a separate string of randomness that is stored as part of the information itself but since all of the information is encrypted, finding out where the private key is inside of the information becomes almost impossible to predict. It becomes even more difficult to predict if you decide to use random string sizes but this is far more complex to develop for a system that is going to be used on a shared network. Now that you have your private key attached to the information and you have your public key, you can then share your public key with the person that you want to know about the information on the list so that they can use the public key to enact the private key that will then decrypt the data that we have been encrypting. This is how a shared list works and it's actually something that has been implemented for a very long time but has never been conceptualized like a blockchain. Instead, this technology has been hidden away inside of something called a 'session'. Whenever you go to a website, you are then subjected to a flood of different types of code whether the person shows Java or python to run their back in script and then how much CSS or HTML, I'm not going to get into any of that. However, sessions are built inside of JavaScript and it is because cookies became so insecure on JavaScript that sessions were developed. A cookie cannot be encrypted unless you manually encrypt it yourself and so it is much more difficult to handle private information via a cookie. However, sessions provided a secondary form of this and what would happen is that the key that is private would be generated every two weeks and the key that is public would be stored on your computer in your cookie. Therefore, instead of needing to constantly login when you were away from the site, you only need to just make sure that you had your public key and that you were in the time frame of the current private key. This would provide a type of session where you would be able to interact with website during the time that these keys were available. However, once those two weeks were up, the public key and the private key would be regenerated so that any bad guys couldn't figure out the information if they wanted to.

This is what Blockchain is

All of this has been to build up the explanation of what blockchain is and give a general idea of how it works but we will get into the specifics in the next chapter. However, we will go over the conceptualized idea of how blockchain works here, and that is to say that a blockchain is a shared list but on a global scale with a key component that helps ensure the validity of the keys on the network. You see, encrypted currency has the problem of the double spending issue. Double spending refers to the fact that digital information can be copied and pasted and so in the past when you wanted to do something like digital currency, not a lot of people understood that the digital currency could literally be copied and pasted and then used twice within the same network even though it would normally be seen as not a valid transaction. It was the definition of digital fraud. Before digital fraud existed, these things included things like identification and paperback money. Therefore, in order to achieve an encrypted currency you would need to solve the double spending problem. To solve this problem, everybody had to have the list of groceries, as it were, so that they could figure out which Keys had transactions at which times. This was to show that the owner of those keys is not, or is the person doing the transaction. By having the network solve the problem of 'who' currently has those keys, you can effectively stop the double spending problem but you need a way for those transactions to be delayed so that the network, everyone in the network, has the opportunity to validate a transaction. This is where the concept of proof of work comes in which will be covered in the next chapter.

Chapter 2: How Blockchain Works

Everyone Downloads the Encrypted List

In the first step of the process, people who receive this encrypted currency will download the list of everybody who has a portion of the same encrypted currency along with their private keys. The way that this list is generated is that you have a worker bot that receives a name and that name is used on the front end, the back end or the middle of the encrypted string that represents the digital currency. Now keep in mind that a blockchain doesn't just have to be utilized inside of currency because one of the key aspects of a blockchain is that it can be utilized with anything that represents digital information, and not just currency. This is actually why this book has been created because a lot of people hear blockchain and then also associate that with Bitcoin, but Bitcoin is just the beginning. So, everyone has to download a list of all the worker bots and their encrypted strings to develop the first array that we were talking about. This is going to be the list that everyone utilizes in order to check whether a person or, rather, a worker bought is the owner of a certain encrypted string. This essentially means everyone is responsible and accountable for the blockchain.

A Transaction Request is Made

Now that everybody has a list of all the currencies on the network as well as everyone who actually owns that currency, they can begin to make transactions on the network, and this is when the second part of our blockchain comes into action. When the network detects that a transaction request has been made, it then sends out a signal to everybody who has currency on the network that also has a current working miner on the network. These worker Bots, which are called miners, then receive the transaction request and receive a block of code that they are going to solve but the problem is that everyone needs to have a chance of solving this block of code and if you have a machine that is capable of solving the block of code faster than everyone else then you run into the problem of falsifying that block of code. Essentially, it is logically possible for an individual to create a network setup that sends a bunch of positive results throughout the network saying that the transaction is valid. But the point of everyone solving the problem is that everyone has a chance to provide an answer from an untampered list. Depending on how many people validate the transaction that is occurring, the transaction will either occur or be denied based on this number of positive results.

The number of random people that are chosen to solve the current transaction problem must be different people on the network that have an equal amount of time to solve the problem. This is based on the power of the network so that the transaction is more secure. This is because if the most powerful device on the planet could be the only person or machine that's validating this transaction, then you invite the shadow powers of the government. Essentially, it would ruin the purpose of an encrypted currency before the encrypted currency ever got out. Therefore, the only two factors that ever provide a confidence level of security in the blockchain are the methods of encryption and how many individuals validate the transaction trying to make its way through the network. The more individuals that can test and validate a transaction the more secure a network will be because it means that there are less people who are capable of fooling the system. The problem is that the system has to figure out a problem that will take everyone around an even amount of time in order to figure out.

A Problem is Determined

Therefore, the very first step in our blockchain encrypted currency beyond dispersing the currency itself and then detecting a transaction request is determining how the transaction will be validated by other users. In order to delay the transaction time so that everyone has an even opportunity to solve a problem, the proof of work concept was developed as a concept that would utilize a delay timer and gauge the difficulty of the problem generated based on the computing power of the network. Keeping in mind, the main purpose of blockchain technology is decentralization, so having a system where everyone works together is key. Therefore, in this order, the problem is generated. A transaction request is made and so the entire network receives a confirmation that the network has received a transaction request. The entire network then utilizes an algorithm to test how much power is on the entire network in terms of computing resources. Once the entire network has generated the difficulty level of the problem that needs to be solved, the problem is then generated so that it takes a specific amount of time for a portion of that computing power to solve it. Once the problem has been generated, the system then chooses a random amount of individuals on the network that will then attempt to use their computing power to break down the problem and solve it. If the computers on the network can solve it during the allotted time then they send a proof of work to the entire network to show the entire network that they have solved the problem and thus the work is validated and by having the work be validated you also have the transaction be validated. The only problem is that if the estimated problem is too difficult for the network or if the network is unable to solve the problem then either the network judged the difficulty too harshly or the transaction is invalid. In most cases, the transaction is valid and it will go through but in the special case that it judged the computing power to be too much then it will repeat the process with a significantly lowered difficulty so that it can validate that it was just the computing power that it misread rather than the validation of the transaction itself. Either way, the network responds to the network with a successful completion or two red flags that suggest that someone on the network not being entirely truthful. If the network responds with positive feedback then the transaction goes through otherwise the transaction is blocked from happening.

A Problem is Solved

However, it's not entirely reasonable to expect everybody just to donate their computer power in order to handle these transactions because the more computing power that the network has, the more security that it has. So the network needs the computing power, but people who have the computing power don't actually need the network. This creates a problem of incentivizing the people on the network to actually do this type of work and this is where the value of solving the transaction comes into play, and why Bitcoin had such a huge impact on cryptocurrencies that we know of. Whenever somebody would get the proof of work problem from the Bitcoin Network, the people who solved the problem would then be able to receive a reward for solving the problem in the first place, and that was usually represented as the transaction fee of the transaction request. The transaction fee was so small that it was almost nonsensical to say that it was unfair in some sort of a way because it was often pennies on the amount that you were trying to transfer. The point of getting into this transaction validation game was to constantly run these machines so that they could solve the problems faster, and faster but this creates a problem with the network because the network judges the computing power of the network in order to generate the problems. So the faster that you actually try to solve the problems, the more difficult the problems get on the network and so it kind of created this self-ending loop where Bitcoin will eventually reach a computing necessity that is far out of the reach of the average individual, or even the Farms that are built specifically to harness this transaction receiving power.

Chapter 3: The Difference Between Blockchain and Bitcoin

What Bitcoin actually is

The reason why most people see the blockchain and Bitcoin as the same machine is because Bitcoin is actually built on the blockchain. The problem is that the Bitcoin machine is not necessary for the blockchain technology to be useful. You see, blockchain can work without Bitcoin because almost everything that I just described could be handled with items such as cars or anything that you really needed to trade on this network. The only problem is that the proof-of-work concept relied on the computing power that the network could provide, and since this was a self-inflicting problem on the network, eventually the proof of work concept would exhaust the network of the necessity to validate the transactions.

A Bitcoin is a randomized string of letters and numbers that represents a personally held value that the people of the Bitcoin Network back with their own concept of value. This is not that different from how the actual monetary system works because a dollar used to represent how much gold used to represent. Gold represented a specific type of Rarity in the world and since a material was seen as rare, it was utilized to represent the end goal of *work value* in the world. However, the United States dollar is no longer based off of what we would call the gold standard, and it is simply based on what we think it is worth in a new form of money, known as Fiat money. The only difference between Bitcoin and actual money is that bitcoin's value is determined by the users on the network without any influence of any type of special body. Fiat money is often determined by both the users on the network, as well as the organization that is in control of printing that money. A perfect case in example is the Chinese monetary system. They are controlling the value of the Chinese Yuan by inflating the worth of their Chinese monetary system, and then deflating it to reap the rewards of making something very expensive or very cheap for other people to buy. This is a very sly and dirty trick that some countries use to conquer other countries without the necessity of an army.

Why the Proof-of-Work

Many people often ask why the proof-of-work concept was the concept that was utilized to help solve the double spending problem but it really boils down to being the first concept in the market in the first place. There are several renditions of this type of concept, and Bitcoin's proof of work simply was the most popular because Bitcoin was the most popular at the time, and still is today. Additionally, Bitcoins were handed out as incentives and were virtually free in the beginning before they started to take on value by being traded and utilized as a form of currency. What the proof-of-work concept did was allow enough time for multiple nodes in the network to solve a problem that involved validating their list of individuals who were currently on the network with those coins being transferred to other accounts on the network. This allowed for the nodes on the network to be chosen randomly, the problem to be chosen randomly, the solutions to be chosen randomly, and the delay time to be chosen randomly. If you haven't noticed by now, the security of this network is based on how random it can possibly be, and so the proof-of-work concept allowed the network to be almost as random as you could possibly be when it came to validating transactions and handling multiple users on the same network.

The Blockchain and Proof-of-Work Problem

As we've already discussed, the blockchain doesn't work well with the proof of work concept because the proof-of-work concept relies on the overall power of the network itself. This creates a recursive problem where the network gets more powerful as the network exists and continues to grow. The more the network continues to grow, the more difficult the problems gets to solve and so this ultimately slows down the entire progress of the network just so that transaction can be validated. This means that the network can eventually become insecure because the longer it takes for computers to validate the transaction request, the more time is allowed for bad individuals to insert their own code so as to falsify the transactions on the network. Therefore, if you can somehow find the open source code to figure out how to predict where the transaction request validations are going to be sent to. You can intercept those requests and then also provide falsified data for those same requests. This allows people to cheat the network at its own game because the network is taking too long to provide the needed transaction validations on the network. This means that, overtime, the network will eventually get so complex at the problems that it generates, that it will eventually crumble underneath its own weight. The proof-of-work concept is really a self-destructive principle that was built into the blockchain without really thinking that the blockchain would become this popular. That's really what it boils down to. The only reason why this problem exists in the first place is that this person who created Bitcoin didn't think that Bitcoin would become as massive as it is now, and it is probably the reason why Bitcoin amount will only ever reach a couple million coins. Now, a lot of people think that a couple million coins is not a lot in terms of money but you also have to realize that these are whole coins we are talking about. If you were to talk about the fraction of the coins, which can go down into trillions, then you are talking about a currency that can literally surpass the amount of money that is going through the United States dollar system. Therefore, you have millions of Bitcoins in which each 1 coin can be broken down into trillions of cents.

The Replacement for Proof-of-Work

There are actually several theories out right now that propose to replace the need for the proof of work. The primary waste that comes with proof-of-work is the amount of electricity that is required in order to do the calculations provided by the computers. Since the amount of electricity that is utilized to do these calculations have begun to reach such a scale that it could require as much power as it requires to power all of Denmark, the necessity of replacing proof of work becomes quite vital for environmental reasons.

Proof-of-Space

One of the concepts is the proof-of-space, and it essentially is another delay tactic that says that a hard drive has a certain amount of space at a certain time. The reason why this is another delay tactic is because a hard drive takes a certain speed in order to read information from it and so when you talk about the space of a hard drive, you talk about how much time it actually takes to calculate the space in a hard drive. This would basically store the numerical version of space that you have left, or you have, on a hard drive where your last cryptocurrency existed. This would serve as the test for the proof-of-work concept. Instead of relying on computing power to solve some massive complicated problem, you would have to guess at the amount of space that the person who is transferring the coin had at the time that they received the coin. Needless to say, this is a theory that is a work in progress.

Proof-of-Time

The second concept that is currently in the works is the proof-of-time concept. This concept is a guess at what time an individual would have received a certain coin. Essentially, a computer would go through all of the different listings of those coins that are available to everyone in the network, and try to guess which coin is their coin based upon time. This would take enormous amount of time simply because the many people on the network really determine how long the algorithm would take. Essentially, you have the amount of people on the network X how many coins are available on the network itself. As you can see, that would be a massive number that would take a lot of computer power to figure out which coin was the coin that is being transferred over the network. Additionally, this type of calculation would also need to guess the exact date that the network detected and when that person received the coin. So you have the combination of the amount of people on the network X the amount of coins that are in the network, and this is then X by how many dates are possible from the creation of the network. Needless to say, it is a different type of mathematical problem but it is so massive that it would take quite a while for a computer to figure out but since it is a simplistic problem to figure out. On the bright side, you wouldn't need the amount of high-power hardware that is currently relied upon in the proof-of-work concept.

Proof-of-Stake

The last section of the concepts that are currently out there to replace the proof-of-work concept, is the proof-of-stake concept, and this is provided by the Etherium network. The developers of this cryptocurrency saw that many people are going to be owning this form of cryptocurrency, and wanted to provide a simplistic solution to the proof-of-work concept. You can simply switch over to how much stake you have inside of the network. This meant that you had a certain amount of coins and you had to prove that you had a certain amount of coins in the network. You prove this by viewing transactions of how many coins that the person was transferring. This relies on something called a lookup table, which is to say that it takes an enormous amount of time to look up information on a table, and the challenging part is that no matter how much power your processing core has, it will generally take the same amount of time to look up the information. Even if you have a processing power that has 8 cores to it, you still have to solve the problem in the same speed as many other people in the network. Needless to say, all of these are very complex in their implementation. None of these have been tested on a very big network, and so the last concept, the proof-of-stake, is a concept that is going to be tested out by one of the big alternative cryptocurrencies. Whether the concept will be better than the proof-of-work is not entirely sure, but the mathematics say that such concepts *might* be better.

Chapter 4: The Benefits of using Blockchain Technology

No Bankers

Perhaps the first real benefit of using blockchain technology is that we get rid of those shady bankers that like to charge us useless fees for unnecessary work. There are so many different fees that are charged by Bankers that don't actually have a good reason to be a charge. I'll just let you know I'll use this time for a miniature rant. I apologize in advance. I mean, really, we have a charge simply for having an account with a company? What brilliant villain thought up the idea that we should charge our customers for being our customers? The insane idea that you must pay a monthly fee in order to hold your money inside of a bank account is absolutely absurd, especially when you know that you can go to a checking account held by a credit union and get one for absolutely free most of the time. I mean, seriously?! What person charges their customer for doing business with them? Then you have your transaction fee. Transaction fees are mind boggling when you understand why these are useless charges. In the old days, a transaction fee would normally require a bank to take a person from their labor force and denote a certain amount of money needing to go to another bank. There was a physical transfer of money between banks in order to validate a bank transfer. This is the reason why things like checks took a couple of days because they had to validate that the amount existed in the first place. When we switched to things like credit cards and debit cards, this validation process became almost instantaneous and didn't require anyone to go anywhere to do anything. All it required was some digital numbers to be changed from one account and then changed to another account. The possibility of physical cash has almost evaporated from the monetary environment, and to charge people to transfer digital numbers that don't require any physical cash behind it is absurd. The bank doesn't have that kind of cash inside of it in the first place, it represents just how crazy banks have gotten with their useless charges.

The invention of PayPal was actually to help solve the problem of why it took so long for money to be transferred between two companies when it could be done digitally. A blockchain utilized with currency has already shown that you can completely remove a banker from the equation by transferring all of your money into the cryptocurrency that you believe in and then utilizing the cryptocurrency as real money. There is no need for the banks to hold the money because all the money is in your hard drive or in somebody's hard drive online. It is heavily encrypted, making it safe so that no one can break into it. We might talk about wallets, we might not, but the point is that Bitcoin has already shown that you don't actually need Bankers in order to complete transactions with money anymore. In the past, Bankers were needed because we all needed a place to safely store our money. For instance, a billionaire does not want to have a billion dollars lying around their house because it is quite obvious that somebody's going to try and break in and steal it. Therefore, a banker was needed in order to store that amount of money in a very highly safe manner so that the billionaire could literally feel at peace with where their money was. Since cryptocurrency is digital, you can store it on a hard drive and since the coins themselves only take up a few kilobytes of information, it doesn't take much space to store the amount of money that you have. This completely removes the necessity of needing a bank in the first place because you can be your own bank again like the days before we created the monetary system.

Real Online Car Buying

There is a rather big problem when it comes to buying cars because the car industry is famous for making it rather difficult to buy a car in first place. For instance, how is a person supposed to buy a car without a car in the first place? How exactly do you get to the place that you need to be at when there are specific locations that dealerships can and cannot be to buy a car? You kind of need a car to get a car. Now, unlike Banks, the reasons why you have to be at a physical location in order to purchase a car and basically go through a week of red tape is kind of reasonable.

The first thing that buying a car means is that you are now becoming part of the population who utilize the roads that the government works on in order for you to actually drive on those roads. In order to actually provide the amount of money that's needed in order to keep up maintenance on those roads. It is understandable to first register your car and then to also tag your car so that each person can donate towards the entire system that helps keep our roads working. This is kind of understandable. The fees for this are actually relatively low in the comparison charts for the past because I remember that nearly 5 years ago I was paying around $60 to $70 and, this year, I paid around $35 to drive my car around. It's actually gone down over time because the maintenance amount is not as high as it once was. With that being said, you also have to keep track of the cars on the roads to make sure that if someone were to steal your car, then you could have proof that it was your car in the first place. You also have to validate the transaction, and finally you have to have insurance on the car most the time. Now if you notice, there's actually no need to go to a dealership but why do they make you go to a dealership? Well the truth of the matter is that you first need to be able to physically see the car itself before you purchase it so that you can validate that the car exists. Well, a blockchain could easily handle this because the entire system is about validating information and if all the cars on the network are cars that are being bought and sold by people on the network, then the information should be valid. The car manufacturers could generate the information about the cars into the system before they are placed on the market. The second step in the process is that you need to provide proof that the car is actually yours, and since the entire blockchain is about being a validity system, then the car would be underneath a system that could prove that the car is yours. Therefore, you have the option to purchase a car that you know exists because it can't be on the network if it doesn't exist, you are able to provide proof that the car is yours because it's on the network in the first place, and you are able to prove that you are purchasing it by simply making a transaction for the car in the first place. All three of these steps make it possible to purchase cars online without having to go to a physical location, like every other product in the world.

Government Red Tape Thinning

Think about how many jobs inside of the government are complex because they need a form of validating that something occurred. You need a bookkeeper in order to validate that transactions occurred inside of a government entity, you need a notary to confirm that transactions of a physical type occurred within a government entity, and the list really goes on to comprise most of the United States government and other governments. The truth is that most of the government's size is due to the amount of validation that the government has to do to make sure that facts are facts. We have an entire IRS for this purpose alone. The appalling nature behind all of these mechanisms needed to validate something that should naturally be true makes one open their eyes whenever they look at the inner workings of their government. A blockchain would remove almost all of these jobs because a blockchain would keep track of any financial tracking that you would need to keep track of. It would keep track of all of your physical transactions because you would only need to upload that information into the network once and then make a transaction of that over the network. Most of the jobs that require any type of transaction validation or validation of existence can simply be done by the blockchain. That doesn't mean that the government will fully rely on it because it is technology, and technology ultimately always has some type of hole in it but since most of everything is digital nowadays, it's kind of foolish to not rely on something like this.

Power to the Users

With a blockchain, the power is finally back in the user's hand. In order to understand this, we have to go back to how we originally began trading things. You would have something that I wanted, and so I would try to find out what you wanted so that I could trade you for what I wanted. Needless to say, this was difficult to manage whenever you had large societies and so the natural solution was to trade in materials for something that represented the amount of work that went into an item. When we switched from using our materials as money to paper or coin as money, we lost control of the monetary system. The monetary system was now in the control of whoever was printing or making the currencies for that system. With a blockchain, we are generating the currency for the system and so the users of the system now have control of the system. Needless to say, most companies that are built on a scheme where they have control of the monetary system don't like the idea of no longer being a business and this means that the Federal Reserve is heavily against the idea of a blockchain based currency. This is because the power will be returned to the users because we are generating it, and we determine its value. Why is this important? If you remember correctly, the gold standard was the only time where the user had most of the control over the monetary value that they owned. When we switched from the gold standard, something set in stone, to the fiat money that we have now. We gave control over the monetary value to the Federal Reserve. During the gold standard time, we had a ton of growth and expansion, but as we've had the fiat money, we have slowly degraded over the years. During the gold standard, we determined our own worth, while the fiat money has allowed others to determine what we are worth.

Chapter 5: The Disadvantages of using Blockchain Technology

A Shadow Currency

The chief concern that comes with cryptocurrencies and the slapstick concern that comes from people who benefit from the fall of cryptocurrencies is the fact that some cryptocurrencies can be manipulated by organizations behind the creation of the cryptocurrency. If someone were to create a cryptocurrency that was sufficient in the job of a cryptocurrency and it had an exploitable hole that could allow an individual to manipulate the process behind the crypto-currency, then you could effectively build a cryptocurrency that can be controlled by others rather than the decentralized cryptocurrency that we all know and love. This would effectively be the conspiracy level of regular money but in the form of cryptocurrency, because instead of a giant organization controlling all of the money in the world, you would have the original creators controlling the money on a cryptocurrency market and deciding who should get money and who shouldn't. This isn't that big of a deal, simply because many people would be able to switch over to different currency networks but it would take a vast amount of money in order to do this if you invested a lot of time in this cryptocurrency network.

Performance

The current problem that we see with most of the cryptocurrency networks is that the performance of the technology it seems to not be able to handle scale very well. This is actually a common problem with the technology world in general because most technology is built for local use and scalability is usually an afterthought until it becomes a problem. A good example of this are websites that are specifically built around handling social media networks. They aren't capable of handling a very large scale. We saw incidences with companies like Twitter, and Myspace, whenever they gained users in the millions and weren't able to take on the load very well. The same thing can happen in a blockchain if you have a method that requires a delay of time before other transactions can happen. Let's say that no other transactions can happen at the same time as your transaction. What happens if you have trillions of transactions coming after your transaction? Are you ever going to be able to get a transaction in? This is the primary concern around performance inside of cryptocurrencies.

Lack of Regulation

While many people love to propagate the fact that the network of cryptocurrencies are not regulated, that is a crutch of the network of cryptocurrencies. A lot of people simply don't trust an automated system because unless the people who are validators have people who validate the validators, then you don't have a chain of responsibility. Therefore, if a network were to be hacked, who exactly is going to stop them? This system is designed to run automatically without the need for a primary figurehead to ensure that everything is running because that is what it means to be decentralized. Essentially, if such a system were to be hacked then you have the problem of who would assume responsibility for taking care of that problem. The same cannot be said about current fiat monetary systems because these monetary systems have their governments held accountable for what happens in the monetary system as well as the corporations who control the influence of money. Since everything is run and operated by the user, it would be the users on the network who would have the responsibility of fixing the network. The problem is that it is the users on the network who may have caused the problem and so the cause of the problem is not often the solution of the problem. As you can see, this... creates a problem.

Massive Energy

We are already seeing this with the proof-of-work concept because whenever you take the solution for validating a transaction to the much higher scale of working with billions of people, you run into the problem of power consumption. Right now, the problem with Bitcoin is that it takes too much power to run the systems needed to validate the network. If you based your system on the amount of power one could generate, you have based yourself on a limited resource because there is only so much power that can be dedicated in the world.

Refusal of Adoption

This is actually a problem that we are currently seeing in certain countries that refused to accept cryptocurrencies. The current cryptocurrency markets are heavily volatile for some countries and these are new technology to these countries that it's simply not worth their time to risk the venture inside of these cryptocurrencies. Therefore, if you cannot get a country to accept the currency then that currency is devalued by the rejection of the currency in a country. A lot of people think that currency is localized and it's worth is determined locally but the reason why the United States dollar is worth so much right now is because it can be used in almost all countries. Cryptocurrencies are not that well trusted yet and so a lot of countries have either put limitations on them or bans. This is because they don't want a type of currency that they cannot control inside of their own country and so the amount of places that you can use a currency also ultimately decides how much a currency is worth.

Maintenance of the Network

When I talk about the maintenance of a network, most people think that I'm talking about a labor force that actually takes care of the network physically. The truth of the matter is that the labor force behind most cryptocurrencies are the people who decided that they wanted to create it in the first place. Normally, they won't stop taking care of it unless they see that it's gone past the point of no recovery. No, instead, what I'm talking about is who is going to take over when there is no more incentive to maintain the network? When you talk about concepts like proof-of-space, proof-of-time, or proof-of-work, you have a network that is dedicated to validating the transactions on the network and so that means that those computers on the network are what maintain the network itself. What's to say that the network will simply see a lot of people cash in their Bitcoins or their cryptocurrencies and just leave the network? What happens when all of that computing power is gone? This is a massive underlying problem with things like cryptocurrency because the worth of the network is ultimately decided by how many people use the network. This problem has the potential to lose trillions of dollars if the industry gets big enough.

If you're enjoying this book, please leave a review on Amazon ☺.

Don't forget to check out the previous books. Check out the Author's profile, https://www.amazon.com/Anthony-Tu/e/B075868KGG/ref=dp_byline_cont_ebooks_1 for more information,

www.wonpublications.com

Chapter 6: Blockchain and the Financial Industry

A Stable Currency

If we have learned anything about our different monetary systems between countries, they're almost always organized by very shady individuals. Let's take the Federal Reserve in this case because there is a lot of hate for the Federal Reserve because of how they handled the issue in 2008. The Federal Reserve reacted to the situation by printing out a ton of money to save people who should essentially be saving our money in the first place. The problem with this is that it sent the entire country into a recession because all of the real estate that was bought during that time simply became worthless because no one had any money to buy any of the real estate and everybody owed money to the banks.

When you have an organization capable of deciding how much money should be released into the market, you have an organization that is capable of making a very horrible decision like the Federal Reserve. Whether the horrible decision was actually a horrible decision or not is up to the philosophers that handle financial transactions but the truth of the matter is that this conversation wouldn't exist inside of a blockchain. This is because the blockchain only deals in what is currently in the market and feeds the market at a very specified rate. This would create the very first fully stable currency that heavily relied upon user activity rather than promises. You might think this is weird but let's go through how your credit card handles the money in your account. It is a known fact that you can run up credit cards and then just not pay them unless you owe close to hundreds of thousands of dollars. It is simply not worth the money to hire a lawyer to go after you when you only owe a couple thousand dollars. It is more money to pay the lawyer then it is to go after you and so most of the time the credit card companies will wait until you actually achieve debts of over hundreds of thousands of dollars where it would be a profitable venture to go after you with a lawyer. Having said that, where does the credit card company get its money? The money itself is nonexistent. The money is money that everyone else is paying into the system and so what happens is that the credit card system is so large that banks are okay with accepting promises for money. Essentially, the bank is okay with accepting an IOU from MasterCard and Visa where the money is going to be transferred into the bank account over a period of time. You can actually set something like this up with your existing bank but you have to have the same amount of credibility as these two massive credit card issuers. Within a blockchain, this is not possible and so defaulting on money is not possible in side of this network. Let me restate that, you cannot default on the money in the network because you cannot spend money that you don't have in the network. Governments that are currently in trouble financially are often in trouble because they spent money that they don't have and now they don't have a way to pay it back and so other countries that rely on said money are fearful of that country might default on the amount of money that they owe. You cannot do this with a blockchain.

Instant Transactions

When you transfer something over a bank to another bank, the transfer is not immediate. It may seem like the transfer is immediate but the truth is that the transfer could take quite some time. What happens is that the company (that's charging you the fee for the items that you have) has sent a digital request to the banking system that you have to see if your account currently has the amount of money needed to purchase that item. Your bank sends an affirmative or a denial based on how much money you digitally have at the time. This does not include things like bills that are coming in or pending requests. With a blockchain, such a request is not required because everything is transferred almost instantaneously to the point where you have a split-second where the money is in the network and then the money is in the account. Once a request has been made with a bank, the digital representation of that money is transferred. That doesn't mean that the money is inside the other person's pocket. What it means is that the bank currently believes that you have that money digitally and the other person got that money digitally. On a physical level, it could literally take a month for that money to transfer into the next Bank. However, for convenience value, you are allowed to make such transactions digitally because all the banks control the monetary system and have agreed that this is a good idea. If a bank were to fail when you made a transaction and the bank itself was to no longer be in business, all of the money inside of your bank would be invalid and so what happens if you made a last-minute transaction that said that you had the money but your bank didn't pay up? Would you owe that company money? These questions don't need to be asked with a blockchain because the blockchain is self-representative and self-validating.

Chapter 7: Blockchain and Other Industries

Financial Records

Pretty much any industry that is involved with keeping track of financial records would be practically useless provided that there was a system that could keep track of the different cryptocurrencies coming in and out. Since everything would be digital, you could easily just set up automated machines to do the work for you and you would just need a developer for that. Since most companies have developers on their staff or can hire a freelance developer, there would be almost no need for positions like bookkeeping and tax experts because you could simply just submit your records via automatic mail and the receiving end would automatically judge what type of taxation you would need as well as what taxes needed to be applied. The entire process would be almost automatic except for setting it up.

New Industries Previously Non-Digital

A lot of problems that arises when it comes to validation is the need for enormous purchases to be non-digital because digital can be falsified. This includes things like buying houses, cars, or anything that costs more than $1,000. If we were to utilize blockchain technology in its full capacity, then all of these industries that were previously not digital would dramatically change because of the rare possibility that an item can be falsified would automatically switch over to a digital version of themselves because the blockchain is self-validating. This would take a process like buying a house, which normally takes almost half of a year depending on what house you're buying, and turns it into an almost instantaneous transaction and all of the different variables such as registering your home, seeing how many people live in your home, and all the different variables that your government keeps track of would be instantly changed whenever that house became yours because all of that information is in your account.

Advanced Mathematics

A lot of people avoid the industry of mathematics but the truth is that the industry of mathematics is vitally important for every functioning device that we have on this planet and yet one of the most boring. When you remove the enormous jobs from the market that require steps for validating transactions, you will have likely removed nearly half of the jobs on the market. The new massive job market would be job markets based around mathematics and since programming, game development, and cryptocurrency development are all centered around mathematics then you would likely have a huge influx of new individuals who seek a higher education when it comes to mathematical theories and the mathematical Sciences.

Court Systems

A lot of the problems inside of the court system industry could actually be solved by the blockchain solution because one of the biggest courts in the court system is the financial court. This is where people argue about how much they spend or how much is fraud in the system or how much they actually did not pay the IRS. In these cases, court rulings would not take weeks to months to even years as they normally take because the blockchain could easily prove the path that the cryptocurrencies took. The only problem would be backtracking where the currencies are in the Market along with where they came from. One of the inventions that the current cryptocurrency market hasn't provided is a back tracking system that allows you to track where the money came from. Since automatic bookkeeping would become a reality for all cryptocurrencies, these issues could be readily solved.

Chapter 8: Ethereum and Other Cryptocurrencies

Here are some examples of different types of cryptocurrencies,

Bitcoin Cash (BCH)

This cryptocurrency still utilizes the information of the Bitcoin blockchain prior to August 1st 2017, but it became its own coin after that date. It's creation occurred because there was a disagreement about how Bitcoin could become faster and this coin represents the side that wanted to make it faster by making the transaction faster.

BitConnect (BCC)

This cryptocurrency already utilizes Proof-of-Stake as well as Proof-of-Work. It is the lending version of the Bitcoin.

BitShares (BTS)

This type of coin is meant for trading in cryptocurrencies, but refuses all forms of current fiat money. This is to preserve the anonymity of the user. The value of the network is due to the fact that it ties cryptocurrency value to objectifiable forms of assets like BitGold, which represents the cryptocurrency of the gold standard.

Bytecoin (BCN)

Bytecoin's sole concern is ensuring crypto-users stay crypto-users and are never identified by anyone via a digital trail. It purposely hides the details of the transactions to keep the transaction valid but hides the users.

Dash (DASH)

This is an Altcoin that is tied to providing better privacy, low transaction fees and transaction times than Bitcoin. There's nothing else that makes this coin special.

Dogecoin (DOGE)

Don't worry, it started off as a joke but it is currently a serious cryptocurrency because it was treated like an internet meme and is one of the top coins. The name is actually designed to rebuke the status the Silk Road gave to Bitcoin and it is based heavily on Litecoin.

Ethereum (ETH)

Ethereum is currently very popular because it extends upon the idea of blockchain further than Bitcoin. It is the most common platform for initial coin offerings (ICO), meaning new coins that are created generally use the Ethereum network.

Chapter 9: Impact of Blockchain Technology

One Step Further Towards a Global Market

One of the big problems when it comes to fiat money is that every civilization has their own form of money. The European Euro, the United States dollar, the Japanese Yen, and so on and so forth. Every single region has their own type of money but with something like Bitcoin or another cryptocurrency, you remove the country's ability to produce their own monetary system. By removing their ability to produce their own monetary system, you remove their incentive to stay isolated from the global community. For instance, the United States government would not normally deal with countries that have no legitimate monetary value to them unless there was a humanity right or need in that section that the United States government felt they needed to step in for. If that country had the same currency as the United States government, the United States government could easily push money over to that country in cryptocurrency rather than physically pushing themselves onto those countries so that they can help. The Chinese market would not be trying to inflate and deflate their current currency to control the flow of currency coming in and out of the United States and other countries. There are several reasons why it's a good thing to move towards a global market rather than individual markets working together.

Further Growth in Rare Areas of the Technology Industry

If we continue to invest in cryptocurrencies, we will see a massive spike in the amount of people that are interested in working in those industries. When is the last time that you met an individual that said they worked in cryptology? Last time I checked, I only met one inside of a movie. I know that this may make it sound like some funny joke that I meant to say but the truth is that this is the truth. The last time I actually saw a cryptologist in person was inside of a documentary about cryptologists. It's kind of horrible to say that that is how I met a cryptologist. Keep in mind that these cryptology industries help protect the information that you're actually going to be using on a daily basis and is the reason why your society is currently functioning in the monetary world, in the cellular world, and in other facets where a connection to the internet is required. These people are crazy important but they are so rare that it takes a documentary to see one unless you happen to be a lucky individual that somehow met one. This is a technology industry that people don't go for as much as things like web development, database management, and other more popular themes because that's not where the money's at, plainly put. A person who is capable of developing a cryptocurrency network has had an opportunity like never before because understanding encryption and being able to improve upon current encryption is what a cryptologist is supposed to do, that's why they are hired. The more encryption that's out there, the more that people will be interested in studying. Then you have areas like online banking, online banking protocol management, and similar almost never heard of fields that are specialized by people who have been in their jobs for decades and that if they die, we have a serious problem. Needless to say, this is kind of a good thing for these areas as it increases the incentive to be a part of them.

A Power Behind Improving Computers

One thing that has definitely stagnated throughout all of the industries is that there hasn't been much of an incentive to improve upon computer design. Most of what powered the computer design era was the ever-present need for better graphics but as we reach the potential maximum for what we can recognize as better graphics, we are making very slow, incremental improvements to our processing techniques and Hardware. Something unique that happened because of cryptocurrency was that graphics card companies began specializing their graphics cards to handle the specific load of cryptocurrency enthusiasm. These customers were after big graphics cards that could handle a lot of calculations at lower wattages. When you look at the average PC Master race gamer, you will not find an individual who is overly concerned about the amount of wattage that their system is using. So long as the wattage amount is no more than a thousand Watts, most Gamers simply don't care about how much power their systems are using and so you had beefy graphics cards like the GTX Titan that sucked up a monstrous amount of electricity in order to provide the amount of quality that the game or needed. It wasn't about efficiency, it was about how much graphical power the graphics card could deliver. What happened when you reached the cryptographic cards is that the companies began to care about the cryptocurrency customers and develop a graphics card that was very high power but at very low wattage. With the GTX Titan you needed a max of 600W and it supplied 2688 cores. With the recently released GTX 1080Ti, you have the same power withdraw but with 3584 cores.

You might think that is simply because of how old the GTX Titan was, but the previous version of 1080, the regular 1080, only came with 2560 cores with only a gain of 100W back in your pocket. This represents the fact that the Nvidia company realized that people who were mass buying their product wanted something that was not only powerful but also something that could offset the wattage required to perform their cryptocurrency mining. Therefore, this represents a direct Hardware representation of how the computer industry tried to change to accommodate these specialized customers. Additionally, many people have seen variant releases of mainstream gamer graphics cards that have better stats because they are built for mining and so these variant cards either provide a lower core count with a significant drop in wattage usage or a higher core count with a slightly increased wattage usage. On top of that, a lot of the new graphics cards are coming in kits that are specifically designed to sell towards miners rather than Gamers because they either sell them in bulk for much cheaper as part of a selection of graphics cards that the company pre-selected to sell towards cryptocurrency miners or they provided an incentive for cryptocurrency miners to purchase those graphics cards so that the mainstream could have access to the singular graphics cards. The reason why they did that is because they know that the mainstream graphics card buyer will likely only by a single graphics card whereas the cryptocurrency miner is probably going to buy several.

A Sign of the New Generation of Technology

Before cryptocurrency really took off, encryption was not on the mind of a lot of individuals and a lot of the concepts that cryptocurrency tackles were also not on the mind of individuals. Sure, things like lessening government control was definitely on the minds before but that's pretty much always been on the minds. Instead, things like transaction security and how to lower the cost of gaming, how to make computer hardware more environmentally friendly, and things of this nature were not truly considered an important part in the technology industry up until the massive influx of cryptocurrency miners. I believe that the current sleuth of changes that are happening inside of the technology industry in the financial industry because of these cryptocurrencies is because it is a sign of the next step in the evolution of our technology and we are just experiencing the beginning motion of this evolution as we try to secure cryptocurrency into our world as a permanent form of currency that everyone uses. I believe that cryptocurrency is going to be the new version of money and that many of our jobs are going to be replaced by jobs that are based inside of technology. This is simply a sign that all of this is going to occur.

Conclusion

Welcome to the end of this book and I wanted to leave off on a topic that a lot of people are interested in because they are unsure as to whether the Bitcoin is worth investing in or if the blockchain is really as useful as people make it out to be. I want to tell you that Bitcoin is likely going to die. Bitcoin was the very first form of cryptocurrency and it was not developed to handle the amount of scale that it is currently handling. The fact that Bitcoin has already sprouted up at least four offshoots of its own brand should represent the fact that Bitcoin has some severe problems. That being said, investing in Bitcoin may or may not be a good idea because Bitcoin does make changes over time and it's really up to the future as to whether investing in Bitcoin is a really good idea. This is kind of how markets work and how stock markets work so you should have expected the standard response when it came to investing but the honest truth is that cryptocurrencies have a lot of room to grow. There is a huge market that wants the benefits of cryptocurrency. When there is a market that wants a product then you know that product is going to grow even though the market may seem a little shaky at first. However, that doesn't compare to what blockchain can do because it is a methodology that can be used throughout several industries. A lot of people think that the fate of blockchain technology is tied to Bitcoin or some other cryptocurrency, but the truth of the matter is that it is tied to the people who develop your technology. Unless you are a developer, you have no control over whether blockchain becomes a standard practice in the industry or if blockchain is going to change the world because it is a tool that already exists and it is up to the developers of our technology to utilize that tool or to not utilize that tool. Let me tell you that the developer community really likes the idea of the blockchain and while there is some criticism behind it, most of everybody agrees that this is going to be a tool that is commonly used inside of the industry.

I hope you received valuable from this book, if you enjoyed this book, please leave a review on Amazon.com. Any review is greatly appreciated and I would like to thank you again for choosing this book. I strive to do the best I can and constantly revise the content.